the commands of Christ

What It Really Means to Follow Jesus

TOM BLACKABY

B&H PUBLISHING GROUP
Nashville, Tennessee

Printed in the United States of America

978-1-4336-7278-1

Published by B&H Publishing Group
Nashville, Tennessee

Dewey Decimal Classification: 234.8
Subject Heading: LOVE \ CHRISTIAN LIFE \ JESUS CHRIST—LORDSHIP

Tom Blackaby is represented by the literary agency of Wolgemuth & Associates, Inc.

1 2 3 4 5 6 7 8 • 16 15 14 13 12

I would like to dedicate this book
to the saints in my various ministries over the years
whom I wish I had been more effective in discipling.
May this book encourage and strengthen you
in your walk with Jesus.

Acknowledgments

I wish to acknowledge and thank my father Dr. Henry Thomas Blackaby for his unwavering dedication to ministering in the name of Jesus to the untold millions of people around the world through his writings, his speaking, his prayers, and his example.

I wish to thank my wife Kim for her unceasing inspiration, insight, and conviction to equip the saints for ministry and serve her Lord faithfully wherever and whenever He calls. Thanks also to my three children Erin, Matt, and Conor for whom I have striven to faithfully model the commands of Christ in the hope that they will also love and serve Christ as they have seen their parents do.

Contents

Introduction

Go, therefore, and make disciples of all nations,
baptizing them in the name of the Father and
of the Son and of the Holy Spirit, teaching them
to observe everything I have commanded you.
And remember, I am with you always, to the end of the age.

MATTHEW 28:19–20

The first few words of the Commission have long been the battle cry of missiologists who inspire us to go into all the world, followed by the evangelists who exhort us to make disciples, followed finally by the theologians who challenge us to baptize new converts and then hand them off to our religious educators to help these young Christians grow in their faith by introducing them to the deep truths of the Bible.

Unfortunately along the way something was missed or unnoticed, something simple, almost too simple. Reading the Great Commission carefully, one notices a phrase that is frequently overlooked and interpreted to mean, perhaps, something that was never intended.

Many churches today are great at going. Many organizations are pretty good at making disciples and have extensive ministries around the world. Most churches are careful to baptize new believers "in the name of the Father and of the Son and of the Holy Spirit." The problem occurs at the next phrase: *"teaching them to observe everything I have commanded you."* Too often we interpret this to say, "Have Bible studies with them," or, "Provide Sunday school classes," or, "Give them discipleship books to read and workbooks to complete." In many cases churches have little to no organized plan for discipling believers or any systematic approach to ground believers in their faith.

What we fail to hear are the actual words of Christ who *commands* us to teach "them to observe [practice, implement, follow, demonstrate] everything I have commanded you." When I have an opportunity to speak to pastors, I often ask them to recall for me a few of Christ's commands. Most often they are caught off guard. Many are slow to respond at first, then after a few moments they begin to draw out some of the passages Christ commanded such as:

- "And whoever wants to be first among you must be a slave to all" (Mark 10:44).

- "I tell you, love your enemies and pray for those who persecute you" (Matt. 5:44).
- "Don't collect for yourselves treasures on earth" (Matt. 6:19).
- "Seek first the kingdom of God and His righteousness" (Matt. 6:33).
- "Stop judging according to outward appearances" (John 7:24).
- "Go into all the world and preach the gospel to the whole creation" (Mark 16:15).
- "Whenever you pray, you must not be like the hypocrites" (Matt. 6:5).
- "Make every effort to enter through the narrow door" (Luke 13:24).

When pastors are slow to respond to my question, I have to wonder how much more so would be the average person in the pew. How can we possibly call Jesus Christ our Lord if we have never taken the time to know what He has commanded? We cannot *obey* His commands if we do not even know what they are. Most Christians want to please their Lord but simply have not taken the time to study the words of the One they call their Master, Teacher, and Lord.

Although the focus of this book is on implementing Christ's commands in our life, I am clearly not suggesting salvation is in any way about *doing*; it is all about *being*. In other words, you cannot earn your salvation by following Christ's commands. You cannot maintain your salvation by doing good works. And you will not lose your salvation if you refuse to follow Christ's commands. This is important. The focus of this book is on what we can do to demonstrate our love for our Lord. Each time we obey Christ, we prove His lordship, and we demonstrate our love for Him in practical and tangible ways. The heart of this book is love responding to love—not duty, obligation, guilt, blackmail, or pressure to act a certain way or run the risk of holy retribution or criticism from other believers. Plenty of eyebrow-raising, finger-pointing, holier-than-thou Christians try to get others to conform to their image of what a "good" Christian should look like. That is *not* what this book is endorsing or promoting. It's love responding to love—that's all.

Not all of Christ's teachings are what we might technically consider to be *commands*. Here are some general categories into which His teachings can be divided. (Examples are provided.)

1. General Observations: "For where your treasure is, there your heart will be also" (Luke 12:34). "You can't be slaves to both God and money" (Luke 16:13).

2. Warnings: "Anyone who speaks a word against the Son of Man will be forgiven, but the one who blasphemes against the Holy Spirit will not be forgiven" (Luke 12:10).

3. Commands: "Let your light shine before men" (Matt. 5:16). "Give to everyone who asks you" (Luke 6:30). "Seek first the kingdom of God" (Matt. 6:33).

4. Conversations: The woman at the well (John 4); the woman caught in adultery (John 8).

5. Teachings/Lessons: Parables such as the sower and the seeds (Luke 8). "I am the way, the truth, and the life. No one comes to the Father except through Me" (John 14:6).

Whether we would actually consider Christ's teachings or conversations or observations "commands," we should keep in mind that God does not give His people suggestions. Whatever proceeds out of the mouth of the Father, the Son, or the Spirit is equally important and authoritative to the Christian life regardless of how we might want to classify it. Christ, Himself said, "Don't you believe that I am in the Father and the Father is in Me? The words I speak to you I do not speak on My own. The Father who lives in Me does His works" (John 14:10), and, "I know that His command is eternal life. So the things that I speak, I speak just as the Father has told me" (John 12:50). So every word that proceeds from the mouth of Christ came first from the Father above. But to simplify things, this book focuses primarily on those instructions that are clearly intended to be commands given by Christ to His followers.

Not all of the commands of Christ are necessarily intended for every believer for all time. Some were given for specific people in a particular situation. For example, Jesus told Judas on the night Judas was going to betray Him to His enemies, "What you're doing, do quickly" (John 13:27). This does not mean everything *we* do must be done quickly. He also gave His disciples power over all demons and diseases (Luke 9) and sent them out to proclaim the gospel, heal the sick, and cast out demons. This does not necessarily mean every disciple for all time has been given the same command. In such cases we will look at the principle behind the commands and its application for us today. Yet I firmly believe the same power and authority Christ made available to His twelve disciples is available to believers today and that Christ may, in fact, direct us to use it in the same fashion in various situations in which He places us.

We dare not presume to put restrictions on what we will and will not allow Christ to ask of us. He is the Lord; we are not.

But what He commands emanates from His love for us. Paul affirms Christ's amazing love when he writes, "No, in all these things we are more than victorious through Him who loved us. For I am persuaded that not even death or life, angels or rulers, things present or things to come, hostile powers, height, or depth, or any other created thing will have the power to separate us from the love of God that is in Christ Jesus our Lord" (Rom. 8:37–39). The writer of Hebrews says, "For the Lord disciplines the one He loves and punishes every son He receives. . . . God is dealing with you as sons. For what son is there that a father does not discipline? But if you are without discipline—which all receive—then you are illegitimate children and not sons" (Heb. 12:6–8). Even in times when God is shaping and molding us, He uses them to develop our character to match what He has in mind for us to do. It is all done from the standpoint of love, true love.

The English language is limited when it comes to translating the language Jesus spoke with His disciples. The range of meanings attending the Aramaic word for *command* can also include "order, precept, injunction, charge, enjoin, and prescription" (Thayer). This means the English word we use (*command*) can also include the wider meanings of these other words. When we think of receiving a command from someone, immediately a military connotation comes to mind, or perhaps royalty bringing forth a decree to their subjects in their kingdom. This is not the essence or the primary intent of the word Christ used. He was not being controlling or being a dictator; He was giving them words of life.

The words *discipline* and *commands* have also taken on harsh overtones in society today, largely because of their misuse and abuse in many homes and families. *Discipline,* to many people, no longer means "to guide, direct, or train"; instead it means to punish or to impose harsh penalties and painful consequences. Imperfect human fathers and mothers, try as they may, are often unable to adequately model the divine intentions for discipline from our heavenly Father.

God's commands may be more easily understood if we look at them from the standpoint of children living in their father's house. Parents have certain expectations for their children: brushing their teeth, cleaning their rooms, showing respect for one another, doing their homework, attending church. These expectations, rules, and perhaps "commands" are not meant to be punitive but helpful in the development of good character and preparing children to be responsible adults when they are out on their own. In fact, it would be *irresponsible* for parents never to teach their children how to manage their money, do their laundry, cook healthy meals, respect authority, be wary of scam artists, or follow God's ways and then send them out on their own to manage for themselves.

Rather than viewing Christ's commands as coming from a master to a servant, a king to his subjects, or a general to his soldiers, we need to view Christ's commands as coming from a father to a son or daughter. The relationship makes the difference. We do not obey Christ out of obligation or out of fear. We do not obey from loyalty or duty, guilt or selfish ambition. We obey because we know deep down inside that Christ loves us and that He has our best interests in mind at all times.

God's commands are meant to help us live a happy, wholesome life that is pleasing to Him and to those around us. What is more, living a life that is pleasing to God brings with it unimaginable rewards. "But as it is written, 'What eye did not see and ear did not hear, and what never entered the human mind—God prepared this for those who love Him'" (1 Cor. 2:9).

Christ criticized Pharisees for needlessly laying heavy burdens on people, and this was not His intention either. Christ's commands were never intended to be oppressive, unreasonable, or burdensome; "For this is what love for God is: to keep His commands. Now His commands are not a burden" (1 John 5:3). Nor were they ever meant to weigh us down or cause us to carry a heavier load than we are able to carry; "Come to Me, all of you who are weary and burdened, and I will give you rest. All of you, take up My yoke and learn from Me, because I am gentle and humble in heart, and you will find rest for yourselves. For My yoke is easy and My burden is light" (Matt. 11:28–30). There is always a best way to approach every area of our life and our relationships with others, and Christ's commands reveal to us just how familiar He is with humanity and with each one of us.

This book is like a plumb line that can be used to assess how well we are following Christ's commands and how deeply committed we truly are to the lordship of Christ. It focuses exclusively on the actual words and teachings of Christ rather than going back into the Old Testament or prophets or supporting material in the Epistles. This way the book becomes exactly what the title says and stays within the immediate focus of what Christ taught.

It is not my intention to diminish in any way the many valuable and inspired commands given in the rest of the Scriptures (i.e., The Ten Commandments) or suggest Christ's commands are somehow superior to them. Christ was with the Father when every single command was given. The teachings of preincarnate Christ are foundational to everything else in the Bible. Followers of Christ could spend their lifetime trying to implement just the commands of Christ, since they give us not only the words of life but also the practical, everyday application of the truth we are to live. This is not a book of rules to follow. This is a book of insights on how to show your love for Christ by intentionally modeling your life after His and following His expectations for you.

As space does not permit individual treatment of each of the commands, selected categories focus on the most complete and clearly understood commands. Upon completing this study, you will have a new appreciation for the importance and relevance of Christ's teaching in your daily life, and as a result you will be encouraged and freshly energized to allow the Spirit of God to conform your life and character into the image of Christ (Rom. 8:29).

1

Coming to God

This is eternal life: that they may know You, the only true God, and the One You have sent—Jesus Christ.

JOHN 17:3

How does one approach God? This question would be nearly impossible to answer had it not been for the Father's only Son who showed us the way. Looking at Christ's life, we see that nothing was more important than His relationship to His Father. His early morning prayer vigils, His frequent treks upon mountains for quiet times with His Father, and His late-into-the-night conversations with God were integral to His ministry. Christ's many descriptions of His Father's kingdom and His Father's expectations for His people were central and prominent themes in His teaching.

The commands of Christ are both instructive and informative. While they give us instructions for life, they also give us information about His Father. For example, when we read Christ's command to "be perfect, therefore, as your heavenly Father is perfect" (Matt. 5:48), we first see the instruction for *us* to live a life worthy of our calling as Christians, but we also see something about the God we serve and worship. So the *command* is also a *revelation.* One of Christ's purposes in coming to the earth was to reveal His Father to mankind. His commands are one of the ways we can learn about who God is and what He is like because they reveal to us what is on His heart and reflect His nature and His character. Each command gives us insight into the nature of who God is and gives us direction in how to come into His presence as children come before their loving parents.

Christ wants us to have a healthy and vibrant relationship with His Father more than anything else. In fact, He wants us to have the same type of relationship with God that He has enjoyed with His Father from the beginning. If you read through chapters 15–17 of John's Gospel, you will see just how important this relationship between the Father, the Son, and you and me is to Jesus.

- "I made your name known to them and will make it known, so the love You have loved Me with may be in them and I may be in them" (John 17:26).
- "Holy Father, protect them by Your name that You have given Me, so that they may be one as We are one" (John 17:11).

- "As the Father has loved Me, I have also loved you. Remain in My love" (John 15:9).
- "For the Father Himself loves you, because you have loved Me and have believed that I came from God" (John 16:27).
- "As You [Father] sent Me into the world, I also have sent them into the world" (John 17:18).
- "May they all be one, as You, Father, are in Me and I am in You. May they also be one in Us, so the world may believe You sent Me. I have given them the glory You have given Me. May they be one as We are one. I am in them and You are in Me. May they be made completely one, so the world may know You have sent Me and have loved them as You have loved Me" (John 17:21–23).

The relationship we see Christ modeling for us with His Father is the same kind of relationship Christ wants to have with us and what Christ wants us to have with His Father. Of course, this is because the Father, the Son, and the Spirit are one with each other. As we relate to one, we relate to all. So as Christ, in human form, reveals to us the Father, who is Spirit, His commands regarding worship, relationship with God, and knowing God emanate from His passion for us to know God in all His glory.

In order for us to experience the fullness of who God is, however, we must meet certain requirements. It is easy for us to think we are at the center of the universe and that God should accommodate *our* wishes. This is delusional thinking, if not sacrilegious to some degree. God does not have to meet our expectations, our standards, or follow our instructions and meet our desires. We are the creation; He is the Creator. We follow His expectations, meet His standards, and obey His instructions in order to know Him, serve Him, worship Him, and demonstrate our love for Him.

Entering into God's presence can be likened to visiting royalty for the first time. You will be coached on proper etiquette by one who knows royal protocol and social customs for addressing heads of state or even being in the presence of royalty. You must do certain things and not do certain things. Christ helps us understand through His commands what is expected of us, how we are to approach our Heavenly Father, and what to expect when we are in His presence. One does not need to read many writings of the Old Testament prophets to understand there are serious consequences for God's people who treat God carelessly or with little respect.

A famous photograph of Pierre Elliot Trudeau, prime minister of Canada from 1968 to 1984, shows him spinning a pirouette behind Queen Elizabeth's back during one of his state visits to Buckingham Palace in 1977. This was a well-rehearsed and deliberate act. He was reacting against the pomp and protocol as well as the separation between heads of state and heads of government. The consequences were not serious; however, his attitude of defiance and disdain was clear. Following the commands of Christ regarding coming to His Father will prevent us from being defiant, offensive, or proud as we enter His presence.

1. Repent

- "After John was arrested, Jesus went to Galilee, preaching the good news of God: 'The time is fulfilled, and the kingdom of God has come near. Repent and believe in the good news'" (Mark 1:14–15).
- "From then on Jesus began to preach, 'Repent, because the kingdom of heaven has come near!'" (Matt. 4:17).
- "Jesus answered, 'I assure you: Unless someone is born of water and the Spirit, he cannot enter the kingdom of God'" (John 3:5).

Not surprisingly, Christ's first commands call for repentance. This is significant in that often in today's Christian circles a call for repentance seems to be glaringly absent. Repentance is at the same time an admission to our faults and recognition of God's holiness. It accepts that God's plans for His creation are righteous, just, and perfect; and our own ways are corrupt, self-centered, and will end in destruction. God's holiness and our sin are incompatible and antagonistic toward each other. We cannot expect to come to God on our own terms; we are only permitted into His presence on His terms, and His holiness rightfully requires repentance.

True repentance brings us back in perfect relation with our Creator and allows us to begin again to experience the joy, peace, security, and contentment Christ intended for us, much as a baby rests in the arms of a loving parent. Repentance is a beautiful pathway we travel that leads us back to where we should have been all along. Without the ability to repent, we would face destruction and devastation and have no way of returning home again. Walking through repentance into the kingdom of God and becoming complete as God created us to be in Him is wonderful. Christ also understands our propensity to want our lives to be self-directed. Repenting acknowledges Christ as the One who is better suited and able to guide and direct our lives. Turning our ownership papers over to Christ is a humbling experience. But for us to pretend to be our own Maker is foolish and reckless.

Christ also says we are to "repent and believe in the good news." Feeling sorry for our sins and failures is not enough; we must take another step. We have to accept the good news of Christ's sacrificial death, bodily resurrection, and subsequent reign as true and effective for our own life. Salvation has always been unmistakably attached to placing one's faith in God and His eternal plan for mankind.

As Christ spoke these commands, He introduced His hearers to valuable, life-transforming truths. They may not have realized that the kingdom of God was, in fact, not just "at hand," but it was standing right there in front of them. As He drew near to them, so did the kingdom of God in all its fullness. For them to enter into His kingdom, for them to become a part of His glorious family, they would first have to repent and then believe in Him as "the resurrection and the life." As Jesus said to Martha, "I am the resurrection and the life. The one who believes in Me, even if he dies, will live" (John 11:25).

Application: In all truth, none of the other commands really means all that much if you skip over this one. Our first love response in obedience to Christ is to repent; to reorient our lives to Christ, His truth, His ways, and His authority. Every other command builds on this first command to "repent and believe." For in it you find life, and in it you can truly begin to live as God intended you to live. Have you truly repented of your sins? Have you confessed them, repented of them, and turned away from them? Have you allowed Christ to have authority in your life? Have you examined your life from His perspective? If not, you may need to take some time to linger before the Lord just now and let His Holy Spirit work in your heart and life (Pss. 32:5; 51; 1 John 1:9).

2. Come as a Child

- "I assure you, . . . unless you are converted and become like children, you will never enter the kingdom of heaven" (Matt. 18:3).
- "When Jesus saw it, He was indignant and said to them, 'Let the little children come to Me. Don't stop them, for the kingdom of God belongs to such as these. I assure you: Whoever does not welcome the kingdom of God like a little child will never enter it'" (Mark 10:14–15).

Why a Child?

- Children are eager learners. To them, everything is new and exciting and carries with it great potential. Becoming like a child is to open our eyes again for the first time, to experience the newness of a spiritual kingdom that was around us all along, but we never saw it.
- Children can accept things by faith that adults would otherwise struggle with. Hebrews 11 describes a litany of people who placed their faith in God and watched Him do the miraculous in their lives. They put away their skepticism, cynicism, and disbelief and simply trusted God, placing their faith in His promises to them.
- Children are willing to give others the benefit of the doubt even when things don't always make sense. I read a story

of a father and son trying to outrun a brush fire. Their only escape meant jumping down a ten-foot bluff. As the smoke encompassed them, the father jumped down first and called to the son to jump into his arms, but the son protested saying, "I can't see you." The father replied, "That's OK. I can see *you*. Jump!" The child jumped into the strong arms of his father waiting below despite his own reservation.

- Love is not complicated to a child. And neither is God's love for us. We were created in love, and God's love sent His own Son to die for us so that we could be made right with Him. We simply have to love Him back.
- God is our Heavenly Father, and He is looking for those who want to be His children and who will trust Him to be their Father.

Application: God is not a simple God, but He asks us to come simply to Him, to trust Him, to believe in Him, to love Him, and to let Him guide us as a gracious, loving father guides a child. God is not your support, your partner, your confidant or protector; He is your Heavenly Father who is all of these and much more. There is never a time when He does not want what is best for you, nor is there ever a time when His love is withheld from you. Has God put you in a place where you are forced to depend on Him? Has He removed some things from your life that you relied on or placed your security in? He wants you to learn to trust Him with the simple faith of a child. Where do you need to let go?

3. Love God with All Your Being

- "He said to him, 'Love the Lord your God with all your heart, with all your soul, and with all your mind. This is the greatest and most important command. The second is like it: Love your neighbor as yourself. All the Law and the Prophets depend on these two commands'" (Matt. 22:37–40).

This is a foundational command upon which all others are based. If you do not know how to love God first, any other command will be burdensome and seem oppressive. When we know how to love someone, pleasing that person will become our priority. In all truth, this command is probably one of the most difficult commands to obey because so many other things vie for our attention and our loyalty. Sometimes loving God can be challenging and require great determination and focus. But great reward results from getting this one right.

Jesus was not the first to give these two commands; His Father was (Deut. 6:5). But we understand the Father, the Son, and the Spirit of God were always together from before the beginning so whatever One did, they all did together. This was certainly the foundational command for God's people. Notice the command was not to fear, sacrifice, worship, serve, work hard for, praise, or give; it was to love. It is instructive to us to realize that the "greatest" of all commands found in both the Old and New Testaments directs us to love. This, perhaps more than any other feature of Christianity, was meant to distinguish it from all other religions. Christ knows that for us to strive to love God first—before anything or anyone else—will keep our priorities in the right place. Once we put first things first in our life, the other things follow in the right order. Only a God of love would require love in return.

An angry god might desire obedience first and foremost. A god of war might desire acts of servitude. A greedy god would require great sacrifice. An insecure god might want a massive amount of praise and worship before anything else. But our God wants us to reflect back to Him what is in His heart, and that is love. Once love is shared, then it is a joy to obey, sacrifice, worship, and praise our God because He first loved us (1 John 4:19).

If you find that you are resentful when it comes to giving to God from your meager earnings, or taking time to worship Him out of your busy week, or if your heart does not desire to praise God even in the midst of your difficult circumstances, then you need to consider whether you truly love Him. The Bible tells us that "love covers a multitude of sins" (1 Pet. 4:8), and certainly this is true when God looks at us. So naturally, when we look at others (the second greatest commandment), we too will offer forgiveness to those who sin against us. As we love others in the same sacrificial way in which God has loved us, we please Him. We also demonstrate to others that God is in control of our lives. Only a person who has known the love of God can truly share it with others.

Application: If you are having trouble loving others, then you probably need to look at your heart toward God. An ungrateful heart will not love others properly. A heart that is resentful, angry, proud, or self-centered has allowed sin to compromise your relationship with God. When our heart is right before God, then we will have healthy relationships with others and demonstrate selfless love to those who enter our lives. Have you fallen in love with God? Has He captured your heart? Have you been overwhelmed by His great love for you, His sacrifice, that you might live? God desires relationship. He desires our love more than blind obedience. He always has. Don't just go through the motions in your Christian life; live as one who is in love. If you find your love for God has grown cold, ask Him now to fan the flame once again in your heart.

4. Receive the Holy Spirit

- "While He was together with them, He commanded them not to leave Jerusalem, but to wait for the Father's promise. 'This,' He said, 'is what you heard from Me; for John baptized with water, but you will be baptized with the Holy Spirit not many days from now'" (Acts 1:4–5).
- "After saying this, He breathed on them and said, 'Receive the Holy Spirit'" (John 20:22).

This command, this act of Jesus, has enormous implications. Prior to this the Holy Spirit only came upon select individuals empowered and set apart by God for a special purpose. Those anointed and filled with the Spirit received great revelation from God, were led by God, accomplished incredible things, and experienced an intimacy with God that others could not. But now every one of us who accepts Christ also accepts the Holy Spirit, and we too are set apart, empowered, led, and can be used of God in amazing ways.

Although this command was certainly meant to be instructive for the eleven disciples, the application is universal for all Christians. The Holy Spirit is to us today as Christ was to the disciples. Christ sent them out in His power to accomplish His will. He taught them truths about the kingdom of God and served as their Model and Guide, navigating their way through difficult situations. This is the role of the Holy Spirit for us today. He also reveals truth to us: "When the Spirit of truth comes, He will guide you into all the truth. For He will not speak on His own, but He will speak whatever He hears. He will also declare to you what is to come" (John 16:13).

So in a real sense the Holy Spirit continues what Christ started. His ministry is Christ's ministry among us. "When the Counselor comes, the One I will send to you from the Father—the Spirit of truth who proceeds from the Father—He will testify about Me" (John 15:26). The Holy Spirit serves much like a personal advisor, counselor, protector, enabler, guide, and moral compass to all who commit their life to Christ. Those who are not believers cannot understand the concept or the person of the Holy Spirit. "He is the Spirit of truth. The world is unable to receive Him because it doesn't see Him or know Him. But you do know Him, because He remains with you and will be in you" (John 14:17).

The Holy Spirit is known by several names such as the Spirit of God, Spirit of Christ, Spirit of Truth, Counselor, and Spirit of Wisdom. Our relationship with the Holy Spirit is greatly dependent on our willingness to allow Him control and influence over our hearts, minds, and actions. As we obey the will of God, as revealed to us by the Spirit, our relationship with the Spirit is deepened and enriched. As we disobey what we understand God's will to be for us, or ignore the Spirit's promptings, we strain our relationship with the Spirit, or "grieve" the Spirit of God. "And don't grieve God's Holy Spirit. You were sealed by Him for the day of redemption" (Eph. 4:30). As important as receiving the Spirit is, we also need to be sure we are walking in the Spirit (Rom. 8:4) each day. The apostle Paul also describes it as putting on Christ so that we will "make no plans to satisfy the fleshly desires" (Rom. 13:14).

In Ephesians 4:25–32, Paul describes for us what it looks like when the Holy Spirit is in charge of our lives.

- "Since you put away lying, speak the truth, each one to his neighbor, because we are members of one another" (v. 25).
- "Be angry and do not sin. Don't let the sun go down on your anger" (v. 26).
- "The thief must no longer steal. Instead, he must do honest work with his own hands, so that he has something to share with anyone in need" (v. 28).
- "No foul language is to come from your mouth, but only what is good for building up someone in need, so that it gives grace to those who hear" (v. 29).
- "All bitterness, anger and wrath, shouting and slander must be removed from you, along with all malice" (v. 31).
- "And be kind and compassionate to one another, forgiving one another, just as God also forgave you in Christ" (v. 32).

When the Holy Spirit is in control and expressed through our lives, we will display more and more of His fruit, the character of Christ. To be walking in the Spirit is to be growing in love, joy, peace, patience, kindness, goodness, faith, gentleness, and self-control (Gal. 5:22–23). When Jesus said, "Receive the Spirit," He was saying, "Receive My life in you." When we grieve the Spirit, we stifle the life of God in us. The command to "receive the Holy Spirit" is not something we *obey*; it is someone we *accept* from God when we surrender our lives to Him. When we are "born again" (John 3:3, 7; 1 Pet. 1:23), the Spirit of God takes up residence in our heart and begins the transformation process in our lives, helping us become Christlike in our attitudes, thoughts, and actions. As we cooperate with the transformation process (Rom. 12:2; 2 Cor. 3:18) of the Spirit of God, we become more acquainted with God's Spirit and more readily able to respond when He is guiding and directing us. "Since we live by the Spirit, we must also follow the Spirit" (Gal. 5:25).

Application: Are you aware of the presence of the Holy Spirit in your life? Can you tell when He is leading you and guiding you, teaching you from God's Word, protecting you, and empowering you to accomplish things God has asked you to do? Take a moment to thank the Holy Spirit for His work in your life and allow Him to continue to mold and shape your life, character, actions, and mind so that you are increasingly conformed to the image of Christ (Rom. 8:29).

5. Enter through the Narrow Door

- "Make every effort to enter through the narrow door, because I tell you, many will try to enter and won't be able" (Luke 13:24).
- "Enter through the narrow gate. For the gate is wide and the road is broad that leads to destruction, and there are many who go through it. How narrow is the gate and difficult the road that leads to life, and few find it" (Matt. 7:13–14).

This is one command that seems to be more restrictive and challenging. It begins to hit at our rebellious nature, our propensity to seek our own will over the will of Christ. But even in this command we observe that there is a choice to be made. There are two paths before each person, one narrow and the other broad. One leads to life, the other to destruction. Most people choose the broad path that seems more appealing; perhaps it is much easier, and most certainly more inviting, than the narrow path, at least initially. Few make the right choice. Few choose a narrow path that initially looks lonely, restrictive, and difficult. Yet in the end it leads to what everyone was looking for in the first place.

Much like the series of lighthouses along the treacherous inner coastline passages that mark a narrow but safe pathway for marine crafts to follow, the narrow way leads to life. Those who disobey the pathways set out by the series of lighthouses do so to their peril and to their destruction. Christ gives us a road map, the way to eternal life, the answer to life's questions, the solution to all the questions mankind has been seeking all along; yet so many choose the other way, the broad way. Instead of everlasting life they choose everlasting misery.

The parameters or boundaries for the narrow way are set by the Father's will and Christ's example. Christ defines the narrow way and the broad road. He knows the difference and leads His followers along the path to righteousness and away from the road that leads to destruction. There are no alternative routes to God, no back entrances into heaven; and the definitions, boundaries, and parameters are not negotiable or debatable. There are only two choices: the narrow gate that leads to life and the broad gate that leads to destruction and torment. Both have a beginning point, and both have a destination to which they lead.

Christ knows how narrow the gate is. There was no wiggle room for Him when it came to following the Father's will for His life. When He said, "It is finished" (John 19:30), He knew in His heart He had stayed on that narrow pathway and that He had completed absolutely everything His Father had foreordained for Him to accomplish.

- "I have glorified You on the earth by completing the work You gave Me to do" (John 17:4).
- "Then Jesus replied, 'I assure you: The Son is not able to do anything on His own, but only what He sees the Father doing. For whatever the Father does, the Son also does these things in the same way'" (John 5:19).

- "I can do nothing on My own. I judge only as I hear, and My judgment is righteous, because I do not seek My own will, but the will of Him who sent Me" (John 5:30).
- "For I have not spoken on My own, but the Father Himself who sent Me has given Me a command as to what I should say and what I should speak" (John 12:49).

According to these verses, Christ did not *do* anything apart from the empowering guidance of His Father. Neither did He *say* anything apart from what the Father gave Him to say. His life was given in order to bring glory to His Father. He did not seek to do His own will but the will of His Father. Essentially, at no time did Christ ever work independently from His Father. He joined in what He saw His Father doing, said what His Father gave Him to say, and completed all the assignments His Father gave Him to accomplish.

In John 13, when Christ washed the feet of His disciples, He finished by saying, "For I have given you an example that you also should do just as I have done for you. I assure you: A slave is not greater than his master, and a messenger is not greater than the one who sent him" (John 13:15–16). And in John 12:26, He says, "If anyone serves Me, he must follow Me. Where I am, there My servant also will be. If anyone serves Me, the Father will honor him." All of what Christ did was an example of the type of relationship *we* need to have with *our* Heavenly Father. The road Christ walked on the earth was indeed narrow; it led directly to a cross. But after the cross was glory. So too, when our days are ended on the earth, we have the promised reward for our love and obedience waiting in glory. Christ alone, through His Spirit, will guide each and every follower to know the narrow road that leads to life. This is why making our personal relationship with Christ a high priority is so incredibly important. Without that growing, vibrant, personal relationship with the Spirit of God and the Lord Jesus Christ, we are in serious jeopardy of getting off track as we walk through life.

John tells us, "Anyone who does not remain in Christ's teaching, but goes beyond it, does not have God. The one who remains in that teaching, this one has both the Father and the Son" (2 John 9). Those who truly know the voice of the Good Shepherd will follow Him. Many religious leaders from the past and in society today have gone beyond the teachings of Christ and redefined the "narrow gate" in their own terms for their followers. They have decided that one must approach God in certain specified ways, have the Holy Spirit revealed in a special way, give extravagantly to *prove* their commitment, believe certain theological perspectives, dress certain ways, deny themselves certain comforts, read only from certain translations of the Bible, or follow a hundred other prescribed requirements of their "narrow gate." In essence they put themselves in the place of Christ. They make grand declarations for what constitutes the narrow gate where often the Scripture is either silent or ambiguous. When people claim they have been given definitive answers by divine revelation on things the Scripture is not obviously clear about, beware of them and reject their teachings.

The only way believers are able to enter the narrow gate is to seek and search for the Lord Jesus Christ. The call to "follow Me" continues to this day. We are to follow no man, no religious leader, no author, no mentor or hero in the faith through that narrow gate; only Christ truly knows the way because only Christ truly knows our hearts. "Jesus told him, 'I am the way, the truth, and the life. No one comes to the Father except through Me'" (John 14:6).

Keep in mind, the narrow gate does not represent simply living a healthy lifestyle or abstaining from spiritually harmful activities; it represents salvation itself. Those who choose and remain on the narrow way will be saved; those who choose and follow the broad path will not enter heaven. Christ alone judges who will be given eternal life and be brought to the place that He has prepared for them in heaven.

Throughout His ministry Christ explained how to have eternal life and how He had been given the authority to give eternal life to whomever He chooses.

- "My sheep hear My voice, I know them, and they follow Me. I give them eternal life, and they will never perish—ever! No one will snatch them out of My hand" (John 10:27–28).
- "I am the living bread that came down from heaven. If anyone eats of this bread he will live forever. The bread that I will give for the life of the world is My flesh" (John 6:51).
- "The one who believes in the Son has eternal life, but the one who refuses to believe in the Son will not see life; instead, the wrath of God remains on him" (John 3:36).

In truth, when Christ pointed out the existence of a narrow gate, He was in effect pointing to Himself. "I am the door. If anyone enters by Me, he will be saved and will come in and go out and find pasture" (John 10:9). This is why He is such an authority on the narrow gate and why He alone determines who can enter according to His standards.

Understanding how all the metaphors used of Christ fit together is sometimes difficult, and in some sense it is probably best not to try to fit them all together. Each of the metaphors Christ uses of Himself reveals various aspects of His nature, purpose, and activity (I am the bread of life, door, Good Shepherd, light of the world, etc.). But when this command tells us to "enter through the narrow door," it really is telling us to seek and search out Christ Himself. There is no secret passage only the most devout may discover, no special password hidden in ancient manuscripts, no clever icons or symbols found etched in centuries-old monuments; there is only Christ. John records it best, "This is eternal life: that they might know You, the only true God, and the One You have sent—Jesus Christ" (John 17:3).

My grandfather, G. R. S. Blackaby, was a lance corporal in World War I. During one battle he was told his troop was to cross a minefield, but they would have to wait for the specialist to take them through. When he arrived, he said: "Listen up! You will follow exactly behind me, not one step to the left or to the right. Because if you don't, it will mean your life and mine." Entering narrow doors, going through sheep gates, and staying on challenging pathways depend on knowing the expert Shepherd, Jesus Christ.

Application: Many people depend on religious activity to "appease" God. God never looks for the activity; He looks at the condition of the heart. In fact, when our hearts are not right, He considers all our sacrifices and religious activities an abomination in His sight (Amos 5:21ff). Can you truly say you are seeking the Lord with all your heart? Are you really on the narrow pathway?

Have you been substituting religious activity for your love of God? Has there been a time when the Spirit of God has been directing you and you have refused to follow His leading? You may want to stop and consider repenting before your Lord, asking Him to forgive you and restore you onto the paths of righteousness.

6. Worship in Spirit and in Truth

- "God is spirit, and those who worship Him must worship in spirit and truth" (John 4:24).

Worship is giving to God what He deserves and what He wants from us. We do not determine the requirements for approaching God; He does. We cannot demand action or blessing from God as though He is our servant and we are the master. Not just anyone is allowed into the presence of God. He sets the standards, He determines the requirements, and He makes the rules for what is acceptable worship.

To worship God "in spirit" requires that our spirit must be made alive by His Spirit. We must be born again, revived spiritually, and enabled by Him to come into His presence in the first place. It is impossible to worship a God who is spirit if a person is not first spiritually alive. "This is how we know that we remain in Him and He in us: He has given assurance to us from His Spirit" (1 John 4:13). To worship God in spirit also means that our spirits are responding to the Holy Spirit. We should be able to sense that He is praying with us, speaking to us, prompting us, inhabiting our praise, convicting us, and glorifying God in and through us.

We must also worship Him in truth. Ananias and Sapphira tried to worship God with deceptive motives, and they paid for their mistake with their lives (Acts 5:1ff). "Man does not see what the LORD sees, for man sees what is visible, but the LORD sees the heart" (1 Sam. 16:7). We have nothing to give God that He has not already first created or given to us. He does not need our car, our money, our voice, or anything else we own. He wants our heart, our soul, and our love. The music we sing, the offerings we bring, the acts of ministry we perform come from our heart; and when our hearts are in right fellowship with Him, our actions will show it.

When we come into His presence for worship, He already knows the condition of our heart toward Him. We cannot lie to Him; we can only deceive ourselves or those who see nothing other than our outward actions. To worship God in truth is to begin to see ourselves as God sees us, to let His Spirit reveal to us who we are in the sight of God and agree with Him. To come honestly to God is to admit our insufficiency and utter dependence on Him and realize we can give nothing worthy of Him except our love and devotion. When we truly empty ourselves of our pride, arrogance, and self-sufficiency, confessing our sins with acts of repentance, we are then able to worship God in truth and with all of our spirit.

God desires real worship. Real worship is not always polished and pretty. Sometimes it includes pain and brokenness and raw emotion. David wrote in Psalm 51 that God desires "integrity in the inner self" (Ps. 51:6). How honest are you in your worship? So often our worship is tainted with a desire to be noticed by others, or to perform for those around us, or clouded by guilt over the sin we have carried with us into worship, and is not truly the pure, holy, blameless worship from the heart that God desires.

Application: When was the last time you asked God what He wanted from you in worship? Do you know if what you have been offering Him in worship is even acceptable to Him? Is what you have been giving to God in worship worthy of Him? Take time to prepare yourself for worship. Do not come tired or distracted. Do not bring sin into the worship center. Do not pretend everything is OK in your heart when you know it is not. Do not let the worship leader dictate your worship of God; let the Spirit of God direct how you honor your Lord. Do you need to confess your sin before you begin worship? Do that. Do you need to kneel in the presence of a Holy God? Do that. Do you need to ask forgiveness with someone you have offended before you worship? Do that. Let nothing hinder your worship, or it will not be worship; it will simply be religious activity that is not worth your time or God's.

7. Abide in Me

- "Remain in Me, and I in you. Just as a branch is unable to produce fruit by itself unless it remains on the vine, so neither can you unless you remain in Me" (John 15:4).
- "As the Father has loved Me, I have also loved you. Remain in My love" (John 15:9).

This command identifies the place where our lives and souls must make their home as a follower of Christ. *Abide* means "to live, to exist, to thrive, to function, and to stand." To abide in Christ's love is to live in the total awareness and appreciation not only of what God has done, is doing, and will do for you, but to order your agenda and life according to His heart and His will. More than knowing about God's love or simply appreciating God's love, we must let Christ's love guide us, control us, and compel us (2 Cor. 5:14) to act and plan according to His desire. When we abide in the love of Christ, we are continually conscious of His presence, protection, guidance, blessing, discernment, and passion for those around us. In fact, it is impossible to appreciate fully the scope and depth of the love of Christ in solitude; it is something that is best expressed with others, with His other family members. The apostle Paul expresses this desire, "I pray that you, being rooted and firmly established in love, may be able to comprehend with all the saints what is the length and width, height and depth of God's love" (Eph. 3:17–18).

When people say they are "in danger," "in denial," "in school," "in a midlife crisis," or "in shock," they are not talking about a location; they are talking about a state of mind or describing their circumstances. When we are "in Christ," we are describing our state of mind, our circumstances, and the location of our soul all at once. When we are in Christ, it does not matter if we are in Zambia, in school, or in trouble, our spiritual state supersedes everything. This is how martyrs could face blazing fires, torturous imprisonment, or imminent drowning with peace because they knew they were "in Christ" already.

Application: Do you know what most often replaces Christ as your top priority? What can easily distract you from kingdom affairs? Are you comfortable and secure in Christ's love? What shakes your confidence in the love of Christ? Are you intentionally developing your love relationship with God? Are you giving Him the undistracted time necessary to do that? These are the things that can prevent you from abiding in Christ. Unless you are conscious of the things that would compromise your affections toward your Lord, you will not be prepared to subdue them and reject them when they tempt you away from God. These things are not necessarily evil in and of themselves, but they can be used by the evil one to compromise your usefulness in the hands of God.

8. Remember and Repent

- "Remember then how far you have fallen; repent, and do the works you did at first. Otherwise, I will come to you and remove your lampstand from its place—unless you repent" (Rev. 2:5).

This *repent* is not a repentance unto salvation; it is a turning back from a dangerous course of life and turning to God. The church in Ephesus had strayed far from its foundations of love and became focused on preservation of correct doctrine, eradicating false teachers, and standing strong under pressure and persecution rather than focussing on love. In fact, they had "abandoned" the love they had at first (Rev. 2:4). Now they were in danger of having their candle snuffed out. For all their good deeds, they were an affront to the Head of the church who was going to shut their doors permanently if they did not *remember and repent.* Christ admits that they were partially on the right track, but because they had lost their love, they no longer were able to represent Him in the community of faith or in the communities in which they lived.

As always, Christ's main concern was the love relationship between Him and His people. Christ appeared to John in a vision with the message to keep the love relationship fresh. He was calling His church to do the things they did in the early days of their relationship with Him. Without that, their good works meant little (Rev. 2).

We need to remember our roots, recall our heritage, and reconsider our foundations so that we do not stray too far away from who we are at our core. Sometimes we think we are being dutiful, creative, and fervent in carrying out our responsibilities when, in fact, we have gone far beyond Christ's agenda for us. He does not ask for our help or our suggestions or our opinions. He simply asks for our obedience and our cooperation with His will. His priorities need to be our priorities. His ways need to be our ways (Ps. 25:4–5). His will must become our mandate.

Application: Do you appreciate how far you have come since you first met Christ? Remembering means appreciating. It also can motivate us to do better if we notice we have made little progress in our faith since our conversion. We have more than enough power available to us to "walk and not faint" (Isa. 40:31). In fact, through Christ in us we can "soar on wings like eagles." Repentance allows us to be in perfect union with Christ, to be in a sublime relationship with Him. It is a continuous action that should be at the top of our repertoire as Christians.

2

Christ as Lord

For I have given you an example that you also should do just as I have done for you. I assure you: A slave is not greater than his master, and a messenger is not greater than the one who sent him.

John 13:15–16

If anyone fully understands the complexities, the purpose, the meaning, and the intricacies of life, Christ does. He created it. "All things were created through Him, and apart from Him not one thing was created that has been created. Life was in Him, and that life was the light of men" (John 1:3–4). If you want to know the purpose of any particular object, the best person to ask is the one who created it. Many people never really stop to consider the deeper meaning of life, nor do they make time to interact with their Creator. Some have deluded themselves by thinking life is meaningless, purposeless, and temporary; none of which is true (Luke 18:30). Once you have understood how much God loves you, that He would even give up His one and only Son to die for your sins, the next step is to understand the role the risen Lord wants to play in your life here and now.

The commands that follow reflect the life Christ lived on the earth. He denied Himself, gave up His rights, submitted to His Father's will, and lived by new and more rigid standards than any religious leader before Him. Essentially, He modeled for us what He expects of us. Following Him means walking in His footsteps, experiencing what He experienced, feeling what He felt. This is possible because He now lives in us. He walks with us, goes with us, guides our footsteps, our thoughts, our actions, and impacts our feelings and understandings as we abide in Him. There is no adequate way to describe this relationship; it must be experienced.

For the Christian, the follower of Christ, His lordship must be the overarching theme of life. Christ's commands reveal that the requirements to be a disciple of His are demanding and require not only transformational thinking but a complete shift in one's life direction, priorities, values, goals, and eternal destination. To neglect these commands essentially means you cannot legitimately claim that Christ is your Lord. He is *the* Lord, but He is only *your* Lord if you submit to His lordship. The most obvious indication that this has happened is if you follow His commands. His commands regarding His lordship are central to the Christian life. The truth of the matter is, if you cannot or will not submit to His lordship, you cannot have eternal life either.

1. Deny Yourself

- "The person who loves father or mother more than Me is not worthy of Me; the person who loves son or daughter more than Me is not worthy of Me. And whoever doesn't take up his cross and follow Me is not worthy of Me. Anyone finding his life will lose it, and anyone losing his life because of Me will find it" (Matt. 10:37–39; also Luke 14:26–27).
- "Then Jesus said to His disciples, 'If anyone wants to come with Me, he must deny himself, take up his cross, and follow Me'" (Matt. 16:24).
- "Summoning the crowd along with His disciples, He said to them, 'If anyone wants to be My follower, he must deny himself, take up his cross, and follow Me'" (Mark 8:34).
- "Then He said to them all, 'If anyone wants to come with Me, he must deny himself, take up his cross daily, and follow Me'" (Luke 9:23).

This command is more of a *requirement* for each and every person who wishes to follow Christ. It is a prerequisite for discipleship. Unfortunately many people choose to see this as a suggestion, a goal, or something to aspire to when they become more mature as believers in Christ. But it is not a command that follows salvation or that comes after being born again; it is a command and a requirement that *accompanies* salvation and a decision that precedes your commitment to Christ. In other words, a person cannot truly be a disciple of Christ until he or she is willing to "deny himself, take up his cross daily, and follow" Christ. Why is this command preached so seldom? It certainly is referenced in sermons, but it is rarely spoken of as Christ intended. It is as though church leaders realize the average church member is generally incapable of following this command, so we bring it up from time to time as a reminder to what we should aspire to do.

The import of this command is that those Christians sitting in the pews each week who do not daily deny themselves, take up their crosses, and follow Christ are self-deluded if they think they are disciples of Christ. Yet many churches seem comfortable with that. If we say,

- "I am not ready yet to take up my cross daily."
- "I am too weak to deny myself anything."
- "The Christian life is too hard to follow exactly as Christ commands."
- "He loves me just the way I am."

then we have changed His command from what He intends to what we are comfortable with.

In many countries today and throughout history, becoming a Christian was equivalent to a death sentence. Converting to Christianity, becoming a follower of Christ, was (and in some cases, still is) punishable by death or, at minimum, a lengthy prison sentence. To claim Christ as Lord during the days of the Roman Empire, was to deny Caesar was lord, which could literally mean facing death on a cross. To give your life to Christ was to take it away from other gods who previously held claim over you. To claim Christ as your Savior could mean to pack your bags and leave your family, friends, relatives, job, and security because you are rejecting their religious beliefs in other gods. Becoming a disciple of Christ means dying to an old way of life and living with a new Lord, in a new kingdom, with a new spiritual family, and separating from those things that are offensive to God. A father in the Middle East today, if found to be a Christian, can have his family taken from him, his job taken away, and be sent to prison until he recants his faith in Christ. Such is the cross many believers today must take up if they choose to be a disciple of Christ.

The Western church knows little about such sacrifice and commitment to Christ. We think we are mistreated if we have to give up a golf game on Sunday in order to go to church. We resent that we cannot sleep in on our only day off. We complain if the preacher goes fifteen minutes overtime in the service. We know little of true denial of self or sacrifice in order to accept the lordship of Christ.

Application: What did you give up when you became a disciple of Christ? What does it mean for you to deny self? Has God's Spirit pinpointed anything in your life that you know He wants you to release so that your commitment to Him is not compromised or jeopardized in any way?

2. Take Up My Yoke and Learn from Me

- "All of you, take up My yoke and learn from Me, because I am gentle and humble in heart, and you will find rest for yourselves" (Matt. 11:29).

I do not believe Christ gives *suggestions* for us to decide whether or not we will abide by them. Christ only tells us truth that He expects us to live by. In other words, we need to reorient our lives to come in line with whatever Christ teaches so that we can truly experience the life He means us to live. Here He tells us to take *His* yoke upon us and learn from *Him.*

This is an agricultural expression whereby one or two oxen or strong animals were guided by a wooden beam that went across the top of their necks and in front of their torso. A plow was connected to the beam, followed by the farmer who determined the direction and depth of the plow while holding the reins to guide the oxen. It was exhausting work, particularly if the ground was hard or full of stones or the weather was hot and humid. A yoke could also refer to a wooden beam carried across the shoulders of a person with pails attached to each end. The yoke was a guiding tool and a working tool. It also signified ownership of animals.

Biblically, the yoke has been symbolic of the bondage of slavery (Lev. 26:13; Deut. 28:48), afflictions or crosses (Lam. 3:27), and the punishment of sin (Lam. 1:14). Here, Christ offers us a new kind of yoke. His yoke is one of ownership; one of rest, peace, and joy; and one of submission to Him as Lord. He explains that His is not difficult or burdensome; and in fact, because He is gentle and humble in heart, we will actually not need to rest *after* our work is done, but the work itself will bring the much needed rest. Serving Christ will be a joy and a pleasure, not a burden or drudgery. Willingly allowing Christ to guide us and teach us brings the meaning and direction we are seeking in life.

Application: Submission to anyone in authority is always a challenge. Humbling ourselves before another takes great composure and courage. But knowing it is Christ to whom we are submitting, One that loves us deeply and always has our best interests in mind, makes it easier to do. Humbling ourselves before Christ gives Him the opportunity to lift us up, to give us strength, courage, and purpose, and help us fulfill our destiny.

3. Follow Me

- "'Follow Me,' He told them, 'and I will make you fish for people!'" (Matt. 4:19).
- "But Jesus told him, 'Follow Me, and let the dead bury their own dead'" (Matt. 8:22).
- "My sheep hear My voice, I know them, and they follow Me" (John 10:27).
- "'Lord,' Simon Peter said to Him, 'where are You going?' Jesus answered, 'Where I am going you cannot follow Me now, but you will follow later'" (John 13:36).

Being a follower of Christ is no easy task, but following Christ is what being a Christian is all about. It is important to examine exactly what *follow* means. It is so much more than intellectual assent or agreement in principle with the teachings of Christ. It is more than living a life that is generally in line with His values and philosophy. The disciples did not just "follow" Christ's teachings; they actually got up from where they were, left their livelihoods as tax collectors and fishermen, and literally followed wherever He went.

Many people want to "follow" Christ's example by being nice to others and morally good, but they want to live their lives on their own terms regardless of any expectations the One they call their Lord and Savior may have. Such people set their own terms for their discipleship and have not taken the time to investigate what Christ's expectations are for those who follow Him. Anyone who tried to follow Christ on his or her own terms in the Bible was a disappointment to Christ and not worthy of being one of His followers.

- "Then He said to another, 'Follow Me.' 'Lord,' he said, 'first let me go bury my father'" (Luke 9:59).
- "Another also said, 'I will follow You, Lord, but first let me go and say good-bye to those at my house'" (Luke 9:61).

At the outset these two fellows seemed to have reasonable requests, but looking deeper, we see them to be mere excuses for not obeying the Master. Whenever there is an "I will, but . . . ," there is a halfhearted disciple. Christ was going one direction, and they were intent on first going a completely opposite direction.

As those who died were normally buried the same day, the first man more likely meant his father was soon dying and until his obligations as a son were completed, he could not follow Christ. Christ's answer suggests others could discharge these duties on the man's behalf, so the question that remained was just how committed *was* this man to following Christ? The second man was in jeopardy of being influenced away from following Christ by his family and friends back home. Too many who "just want to say good-bye," after doing so, never return to follow what Christ asked them to do because of the persuasive powers of their nonbelieving friends and family.

Another man sought to follow Christ on his own terms, but Christ, seeing the man's heart, pressed him further. "'If you want to be perfect,' Jesus said to him, 'go, sell your belongings and give to the poor, and you will have treasure in heaven. Then come, follow Me.' When the young man heard that command, he went away grieving, because he had many possessions" (Matt. 19:21–22). Here again something stood between the man and following Christ.

- "And whoever doesn't take up his cross and follow Me is not worthy of Me" (Matt. 10:38).
- "Then Jesus said to His disciples, 'If anyone wants to come with Me, he must deny himself, take up his cross, and follow Me'" (Matt. 16:24).

Those who do not follow Christ on Christ's terms are not truly following Christ at all. They are perhaps *investigating* Christ, or *admiring* Christ, or *studying* Christ, or *curious* about Christ, but the commitment to *follow* Him is not there. True following supersedes any family obligation, all other earthly relationships, and any other priority in life one may have. This never means that we are to treat our parents callously or be deliberately unkind to our friends or family. It is sad to see people acting harshly and carelessly toward those who truly love them in order to follow what they believe Christ has called them to do. Christ showed such an amazing love for us, and yet people can be so unloving to their own family members. It is rarely necessary to abandon or turn our backs on our family and friends in order to follow Christ; we need to be Christ's ambassadors and God's agents of reconciliation to draw them to Christ with the same love that drew us. "Christ's love compels us" (2 Cor. 5:14) to treat and speak to everyone just as He would treat and speak to them.

To follow Christ may mean leaving your present vocation (as it did Peter, James, John, Matthew, and the other disciples), adjusting your own dreams and personal goals to be in line with His will (as in the life of apostle Paul), and taking on challenges you never before considered. Following Christ may also mean going back to your own hometown and family to share the good news you have found, as in this account from Christ's ministry:

> As He was getting into the boat, the man who had been demon-possessed kept begging Him to be with Him. But He would not let him; instead, He told him, "Go back home to your own people, and report to them how much the Lord has done for you and how He has had mercy on you." So he went out and began to proclaim in the Decapolis how much Jesus had done for him, and they were all amazed. (Mark 5:18–20)

Remember, whether it means leaving everyone and everything you have known or returning back to your own family and colleagues, Christ sets the terms, not us, of what following Him means. Don't assume that your following of Christ will look like other followers around you.

Application: Are you sure that you are truly following Christ, or are you simply curious or investigating Christ? Can you look back over your life to see where you have had to leave certain things, change your priorities, or reorient your goals to bring them in line with where Christ was going in your life? If you can see no significant difference from before you met Christ until now, you have good reason to ask whether you are truly following Him or He has gone on ahead without you.

4. You Have Heard It Said . . . but I Say to You

- "You have heard that it was said, An eye for an eye and a tooth for a tooth. But I tell you, don't resist an evildoer. On the contrary, if anyone slaps you on your right cheek, turn the other to him also" (Matt. 5:38–39).

This command is included in a series of exhortations Christ left with His people. He first provides us with the traditional views of how people related to others:

- "Do not murder, and whoever murders will be subject to judgment" (Matt. 5:21).
- "Do not commit adultery" (Matt. 5:27).
- "Whoever divorces his wife must give her a written notice of divorce" (Matt. 5:31).
- "You must not break your oath, but you must keep your oaths to the Lord" (Matt. 5:33).

And then He gives us His corresponding version of how we are to relate to those around us:

- "But I tell you, everyone who looks at a woman to lust for her has already committed adultery with her in his heart" (Matt. 5:28).
- "But I tell you, everyone who is angry with his brother will be subject to judgment. And whoever says to his brother,

'Fool!' will be subject to the Sanhedrin. But whoever says, 'You moron!' will be subject to hellfire" (Matt. 5:22).

- "But I tell you, everyone who divorces his wife, except in a case of sexual immorality, causes her to commit adultery. And whoever marries a divorced woman commits adultery" (Matt. 5:32).
- "But I tell you, don't take an oath at all: either by heaven, because it is God's throne; or by the earth, because it is His footstool; or by Jerusalem, because it is the city of the great King. Neither should you swear by your head, because you cannot make a single hair white or black. But let your word 'yes' be 'yes,' and your 'no' be 'no.' Anything more than this is from the evil one" (Matt. 5:34–37).

We need to do some things to demonstrate we belong to Christ. We must rise above the ordinary and traditional views of being politically correct or socially responsible and take on Christ's much more comprehensive behaviors and attitudes. We are measured by a different standard, not simply by visible adherence to a law or rule but by the inner attitudes of love and grace, the motives and condition of the heart. When we entered into His kingdom, we joined a new team; we became "a chosen race, a royal priesthood, a holy nation, a people for His possession." He calls us "out of darkness into His marvelous light" (1 Pet. 2:9). We can no longer live business as usual in the world because our objectives and purpose in life have been radically altered forever. To try to live our own life with our own goals and our own priorities flies in the face of Christ, who gave His life for us so that He might now live through us.

Application: Have you accepted Christ's standard of conduct for His people? Have you acquiesced to His expectations for you personally? Your answer to these questions reveals whether Christ is truly your Lord. When Christ's commands become integrated into your lives to the point that they become a part of your nature, you will not only begin reflecting Christ to others, but He will be accomplishing His work through you on the earth.

5. Pray This Way

- "Therefore, you should pray like this: Our Father in heaven, Your name be honored as holy. Your kingdom come. Your will be done on earth as it is in heaven" (Matt. 6:9–10).

The disciples had observed Jesus praying in many different places and on many different occasions. This command was a response to their request that Jesus teach them to pray. Christ not only took time to point out the hypocrisy that was prevalent among His people regarding their prayers, but He offered a new way to pray, a model prayer for those who wanted to seek God but did not know how.

There was a shortage of good models for prayer, and their religious leaders seemed to have lost their way in knowing how to relate to God. So Christ showed them the manner in which He talked to His Father. Although God had previously referred to Himself as the Father of Israel (Jer. 31:9; Mal. 1:6), Jesus' hearers likely had never considered calling God "Father" in their prayers. They were not used to being so intimate and personal with their Creator. Christ's command again reveals much about God.

Christ's prayer begins with acknowledging the character of the One to whom they were speaking. "Our Father, hallowed or holy is your name." Then the people heard that God is indeed interested in their daily needs of provisions and protection. They heard about His will and His kingdom, about forgiveness, and about helping us deal with temptation. Many of these things children could have asked of their earthly fathers or mothers. In this command, Christ brings Almighty God into the perspective of a loving Father who is interested in His children.

This is not a prayer that depends on "vain repetitions" (Matt. 6:7 KJV) or verbosity, lofty words, and religious clichés. It shows humility, directness, respect, and proper focus—things not found in the prayers of the hypocrites. This command is neither limiting and nor does it create unreasonable expectations and place burdens on our backs. It is freeing, refreshing, almost exciting to know we can talk with God personally and intimately.

Application: When you pray, do not imitate other people; simply talk with your Lord and your God as one friend talks to another. Keep it simple, honest, and respectful. Leave room for God's Spirit to reply to you. Pray with anticipation and excitement because the God of the universe enjoys talking with you one-on-one and showing you great and mighty things you would never otherwise know.

6. Do This in Remembrance of Me

- "This is My body, which is given for you. Do this in remembrance of Me" (Luke 22:19).

At a crossroads near my home, a simple wooden cross has been erected. A small brass plaque in the center explains why. It was put there in memory of a young man who died in a car accident at that spot. Underneath the cross is a container that is regularly filled with flowers, and a small flower bed has been planted that is beautifully tended. Each time I pass that cross, I am reminded of the fragility of life and the love of a family determined not to let the young man who died there be forgotten.

In similar fashion, Christ gives us this command: "Do this in remembrance of Me." Do not allow the sacrifice I made, the price I paid, to be forgotten or taken for granted. This act is one of two commands pertaining to worship that are universally accepted in the Christian church.

It is called by many names: the Lord's Supper, Holy Communion, the Eucharist, the Blessed Sacrament; but Communion stands out in the commands of Christ because it is something Christ requires His people to do as an act of worship. It is like a memorial of remembrance whereby we set aside focused time to reflect on the sacrifice of Christ and to honor His obedience to His Father in heaven. People do this in a myriad of ways. There is a wide range of variations on when (or how often) it can be done (weekly, monthly, quarterly), by whom it can be done (ordained minister or layperson), what elements are used (bread, wafers, crackers, wine, grape juice), what it means exactly (remembrance, confession, recommitment, empowerment), and how symbolic it is. Regardless of any of these variations, it is still done today as it was in the past, in obedience to the command of Christ.

Jesus' sacrifice on the cross was the most important act of obedience He performed in His short life on the earth. It was the reason He came in the first place. Through His death Christ created a bridge over which mankind is able to be reconciled to God. To neglect observing Communion is to declare Christ's death as unimportant and insignificant.

Paul gives us the reason for celebrating the Lord's Supper as well as a caution, "For as often as you eat this bread and drink the cup, you proclaim the Lord's death until He comes. Therefore, whoever eats the bread or drinks the cup of the Lord in an unworthy way will be guilty of sin against the body and blood of the Lord. So a man should examine himself; in this way he should eat the bread and drink from the cup" (1 Cor. 11:26–28).

We proclaim the Lord's death until He comes, but we also proclaim that we serve a living Lord who was, is, and is coming (Rev. 1:8). To dishonor or neglect this command can have serious consequences for Christians. "So Jesus said to them, 'I assure you: Unless you eat the flesh of the Son of Man and drink His blood, you do not have life in yourselves'" (John 6:53).

Application: Observing Communion should never be done lightly. It is a deeply meaningful and personal action done by Christ's followers in honor of His sacrifice for our sins. For this rite to become a ritual, a mindless habit, or a religious duty is no different than to neglect doing it at all. Each person should take time to examine themselves and let the Spirit of God examine them as David prayed, "Search me, God, and know my heart; test me and know my concerns. See if there is any offensive way in me; lead me in the everlasting way" (Ps. 139:23–24). We must at the same time reflect on the extent to which we have also taken up our cross and followed Him. We should also take time to recommit our lives to being "a living sacrifice" (Rom. 12:1) for His service and His kingdom.

7. Remember What I Said

- "Remember the word I spoke to you: 'A slave is not greater than his master.' If they persecuted Me, they will also persecute you. If they kept My word, they will also keep yours" (John 15:20).

Maybe this seems like a strange command at first: to remember Christ's commands. But Christ knows His people all too well. We are forgetful, easily distracted, fickle, neglectful, and rebellious. Jesus knew He would only be physically present with His disciples for a while longer. He had so much to teach them, and they were to be charged with a great task: to take the gospel to the world. It was important that they remember His words.

These are the words they would teach others. These are the words they would record in the Gospels so we also could hear and remember. Christ reminds us how important it is to remember His words because His words are life and they keep us securely in His will. Sometimes remembering His Word will help us answer questions that arise at a later time, or will keep us from straying, just as when Christ met the devil's temptations with Scripture. Remembering His words is remembering He is with us and in us and that His words have power to accomplish His will in and through our lives.

The words of Christ are powerful. At His word, stormy seas were calmed. At His word, healing occurred. At His word, what was once dead was restored to life. Jesus' words contain the same power today. The words of Christ have power to heal, to restore, and to bring life. Like the disciples those many years ago, we are charged with remembering and sharing these words. Do we know them? Will we remember? To whom are we sharing His words?

- "Heaven and earth will pass away, but My words will never pass away. Be on your guard, so that your minds are not dulled from carousing, drunkenness, and worries of life, or that day will come on you unexpectedly like a trap. For it will come on all who live on the face of the whole earth. But be alert at all times, praying that you may have strength to escape all these things that are going to take place and to stand before the Son of Man" (Luke 21:33–36).

Application: Do you take time to hide His words in your heart? Do you have a plan for Scripture memory and meditation on God's Word? It will be difficult for you to remember words you have not even read or words you have not examined or thoughtfully considered. Keep in mind that the words of Christ can be the difference between life and death, victory or defeat, and success or failure.

3

Character

I wrote for this purpose: to test your character
to see if you are obedient in everything.

2 Corinthians 2:9

But put on the Lord Jesus Christ, and make
no plans to satisfy the fleshly desires.

Romans 13:14

Our character matters to Christ. How we serve Christ and how we fulfill our duties as disciples is determined by our character. A person with good character will faithfully serve Christ out of love and gratefulness. Those with poor character begrudgingly serve out of duty, obligation, or for personal gain, if they manage to serve at all. Christ is not so much concerned with what we *do* for Him as He is with the condition of our heart because that will determine our character. Jesus said, "For each tree is known by its own fruit. Figs aren't gathered from thornbushes, or grapes picked from a bramble bush. A good man produces good out of the good storeroom of his heart" (Luke 6:44–45). What we *do* needs to come out of who we *are* in Christ. Our actions demonstrate to others who has control over our life. It is no wonder many of Christ's commands center on our character—who we are on the inside—because that most often determines what we will say and do.

Many Christians lose sight of the fact that they represent Christ to their families, friends, coworkers, neighbors, and strangers. People today seem to have a poor perception of what Christians are like because of a poor example they have encountered. A non-Christian relative told me one of the worst employees he ever had was a Christian who was stealing from his company. That man's poor character and bad choices brought disrepute on all Christians and on Christ.

Christ will always match His assignments for us with our character. In other words, the more trustworthy, faithful, diligent, honest, caring, and hardworking we are, the larger and more significant the assignment may be. Over the years I have watched as my father was invited to the United States White House in Washington, D.C., to speak with two presidents. He has also spoken to the heads of all the African countries at the United Nations and been in the offices of various presidents around the world. Not many people have such access to leaders of countries, but God can trust him with these assignments because my father has had a history of representing Christ well in tough situations.

God will place us in various situations to test our character and see if we are going to be faithful in small things before He places us in a situation with greater influence and impact. Character is often the single most determining factor of our usability in God's hands.

1. Walk in the Light

- "Jesus answered, 'The light will be with you only a little longer. Walk while you have the light so that darkness doesn't overtake you. The one who walks in darkness doesn't know where he's going. While you have the light, believe in the light so that you may become sons of light'" (John 12:35–36).

Walking in darkness is difficult and dangerous, and progress is slow. But with the flick of a light switch, dangers, impediments, and pathways are immediately made known and are clearly seen. When we seek the Lord and allow His Spirit to guide our lives, He makes clear to us the dangers as well as the pathways for getting around impediments in life. This is similar to walking in truth or walking with Christ, allowing Him to guide our footsteps, decisions, commitments, and involvement in situations and in people's lives. Walking in darkness always happens when we strike out on our own with little or no consideration for what God's Spirit may be telling us.

Several months ago I was heading home late one night from a meeting at a home in the countryside. It was dark and raining; visibility was limited. I chose to take a different road home that I had once taken in the daylight, but it quickly became clear that I didn't know where I was going. The angles and turns of the roads left me disoriented, and I came to an intersection with absolutely no clue as to which was the right way. I guessed wrong and eventually came to a dead end. I could feel panic begin to well up in me so I tried backtracking, but that didn't work either. Trying one last road, I finally drove by a street sign leading me to the right way home. The next time I went that direction, I had my GPS in the car. I zipped through the country roads never missing a turn and had not a moment of stress or panic. The difference was having a guide in the car.

Each of us is allotted a certain amount of time here on this earth. Our days are numbered, and not using our time wisely is foolishness and poor stewardship of a tremendous gift. How we use our days shows how grateful we are to the Giver of life. Christ's days were also numbered on the earth, yet He was able to accomplish everything His Father had set before Him to accomplish. He could say upon the cross, "It is finished!" (John 19:30), knowing He had completed every last prophecy, every expectation, and every deed He had been sent from heaven to do.

The apostle Paul reminds us, "For we are His creation, created in Christ Jesus for good works, which God prepared ahead of time so that we should walk in them" (Eph. 2:10). Walking in the light is to walk in the presence of the Lord, doing what He has prepared in advance for us to do, so that when we see Him face-to-face He will turn to us and say, "Well done, good and faithful slave!" (Matt. 25:23).

The second part of this command is also consistent with the first, as it encourages us to "believe in the light," and in doing so, we "become sons of light." When John introduces Christ to us in his gospel, he points out that Jesus is the light of men. "Life was in Him, and that life was the light of men. That light shines in the darkness, yet the darkness did not overcome it" (John 1:4–5). Christ's command reveals that prior to Christ's coming, there was only darkness. When Christ arrived, the light of the world also arrived. "Then Jesus spoke to them again: 'I am the light of the world. Anyone who follows Me will never walk in the darkness but will have the light of life'" (John 8:12).

Application: We have a choice in how we walk. We can choose to live in the light with purpose and God's direction, or we can choose to remain in darkness without direction or purpose. The nature of darkness is to overtake you, to confuse, disorient, and prevent you from reaching your destination. The nature of light is to reveal truth, to show the way, to expose those things that are hidden, and to dispel fear. Christ's command, if followed, allows us to avoid the pitfalls that await those walking in darkness. It not only gives us direction in life but also provides us with our identity as children of light. As we walk in the light, we are covered by the presence of Light and are protected from the evil one.

2. Shine Your Light

- "Let your light shine before men, so that they may see your good works and give glory to your Father in heaven" (Matt. 5:16).

After we have learned to walk in the light and believe in the light, we are to let that light shine brightly through our lives for all to see. Our Christianity was no more meant to be private than a light in a room can be. A light impacts everyone within its range. You might try to have your own personal light, or put barricades around it to protect it and limit its influence, but it was designed to dispel darkness and will shine even through the smallest crack.

Christ explains, "You are the light of the world. A city situated on a hill cannot be hidden. No one lights a lamp and puts it under a basket, but rather on a lampstand, and it gives light for all who are in the house" (Matt. 5:14–15). This command causes us to recognize that as we allow our light to shine, we draw attention to the source of that light, which is Jesus. We also reveal the truth (Christ) for all to see. The light of the world is Jesus in us. The hope for the world is Jesus in us. Otherwise, all is darkness. Our light shines as the character of Christ is developed in us and as we reach out to others with the love of Christ.

An isolated life is a selfish life. The light is hidden. A life centered only on my own family is a selfish life. The light is hidden in my house. Our light was meant to shine before men and before the world. To try to hide our light is to deny the purpose of light, and it countermands both Christ's orders and His heart. He said, "If I am lifted up from the earth I will draw all people to Myself" (John 12:32). It has always been Christ's intention to draw all people to Himself. Until He comes again, we are the means by which He will accomplish that end.

Application: What actions are you currently involved in that let others see Jesus in you? Are you consciously shining the light of Christ's love for others to see, or are you trying to fit in with the crowd, or not "make waves," just trying to keep your head down and do your job without being noticed too much? We are not supposed to draw attention to ourselves; we are to let Christ draw attention to *Himself* through us as we live our lives with purpose and meaning in obedience to the Spirit within us. Don't be surprised when people are drawn to Christ in you when you truly let Him shine brightly through your life.

3. Be Humble

- "But as for you, do not be called 'Rabbi,' because you have one Teacher, and you are all brothers. Do not call anyone on earth your father, because you have one Father, who is in heaven. And do not be called masters either, because you have one Master, the Messiah. The greatest among you will be your servant. Whoever exalts himself will be humbled, and whoever humbles himself will be exalted" (Matt. 23:8–12).
- "Jesus called them over and said to them, 'You know that those who are regarded as rulers of the Gentiles dominate them, and their men of high positions exercise power over them. But it must not be like that among you. On the contrary, whoever wants to become great among you must be your servant, and whoever wants to be first among you must be a slave to all. For even the Son of Man did not come to be served, but to serve, and to give His life—a ransom for many'" (Mark 10:42–45; also Luke 22:25).

By the time he retired, my father-in-law had become the vice president of a large company in Canada with several thousand employees under him. Yet, when you came for an appointment with Ted Stokes, you would bypass all the large, impressive offices to find a small corner office that was his by choice. On Friday afternoons you would not find him in the office at all because he preferred to be in the warehouse, working alongside his employees filling orders. Ted believed that it was important to stay in touch with his employees and was not above rolling up his sleeves and getting his hands dirty. When Ted retired, cards, gifts, and flowers filled the house from across Canada. At his retirement party, grown men sobbed as they related stories of the difference Ted had made in their lives both personally and professionally. For Ted Stokes the measure of a man was not defined by titles, positions, fancy offices, or preferential treatment; it was defined in the character of someone who knew how to serve and not consider himself above everyone else.

Christ values humility and a proper view of oneself. In some countries and in some cultures, having titles is important. In India and Africa you receive much respect and prestige if you are called "doctor" or "reverend" or even "pastor"; but in the eyes of Christ, we are all on equal ground and none is above the other. We are all brothers and sisters, fellow travellers on the road, all walking together in the kingdom of God.

It is OK to be honored by people if you have served them well, but to *expect* special treatment from others, or to desire to be served before everyone else, or to have the best seats in the house, or not to have to deal with restrictions other people must deal with is selfish and self-centered. If we are always looking to our own needs, then we are not conscious of others' needs. Paul reminds us, "Do nothing out of rivalry or conceit, but in humility consider others as more important than yourselves. Everyone should look out not only for his own interests, but also for the interests of others" (Phil. 2:3–4).

Be careful to understand that these commands do not nullify the command to "honor your father and your mother" (Exod. 20:12). Nor are they requiring us to be disrespectful toward those in authority over us. These commands place our Lord and our God in His rightful place of preeminence in our life and above all else.

This command also reflects Christ's own actions and heart. The apostle Paul demonstrated this aspect of leadership in his own ministry and admonished us:

> Make your own attitude that of Christ Jesus, who, existing in the form of God . . . emptied Himself by assuming the form of a slave, taking on the likeness of men. . . . He humbled Himself by becoming obedient to the point of death—even to death on a cross. For this reason God highly exalted Him and gave Him the name that is above every name, so that at the name of Jesus every knee will bow—of those who are in heaven and on earth and under the earth—and every tongue should confess that Jesus Christ is Lord, to the glory of God the Father. (Phil. 2:5–11)

What is consistent about Christ's commands is that He doesn't just *command* us to humble ourselves, to serve one another, and to consider others as greater than ourselves; He actually *demonstrates* how to do it. The typical leadership model most people were used to was a person who gained authority over others, then continually reminded them of their subservience to their leader. They were used to leaders being served, not serving. They were used to bowing before leaders or looking up to them as they sat in their places of honor, not looking down on them as they stooped to wash the dirty feet before them (John 13:5). Jesus modeled for us what it meant to be great and important in God's kingdom as He knelt to wash the disciples' feet. He demonstrated true humility when He, the God of the universe, became a helpless baby and submitted to the humiliation and savagery of a criminal's death on the cross. Jesus gave up position, authority, reputation, and power in obedience to the Father; and yet we question why someone else should receive more privileges than we do.

The principle behind the command is that those who are courageous enough to humble themselves before others have the good character and moral fiber God can trust to lead others. Those who demand subservience from others have let pride and selfish ambition corrupt their character. They show contempt toward others and can in no way represent the heart of God. Christ tells us that "the gentle . . . will inherit the earth" (Matt. 5:5).

Application: Jesus wants all His brothers and sisters to have a family resemblance. He does not want His people to look like the world because we no longer belong to the kingdom of this world. Being humble is a reflection of Christ in us. We no longer need to draw attention to ourselves, but we love to draw attention to Christ who saved us, transformed us, and now lives in us.

4. Be Merciful

- "Be merciful, just as your Father also is merciful" (Luke 6:36).
- "The merciful are blessed, for they will be shown mercy" (Matt 5:7).

Showing mercy is a reflection of the heart of God. Grace is giving us what we do not deserve. Mercy, in essence, is withholding the punishment we rightly deserve. When we are merciful to others, we are acting like God acts. "The LORD is merciful and gracious, slow to anger, and plenteous in mercy" (Ps. 103:8 KJV).

- When the angel of God took Lot and his wife by the hand and forced them out of the city before Sodom and Gomorrah were consumed by fire, God showed them mercy (Gen. 19:16).
- When Paul and Silas told their Philippian jailor to put away his sword and do himself no harm, they showed mercy toward their abuser (Acts 16:28).
- When David had opportunity to take his revenge upon Saul's life but chose not to, he showed mercy (1 Sam. 24:7).
- When the rich master chose to forgive the debt of his servant rather than casting him into debtor's prison, he showed mercy (Matt. 18:27).

- When Jesus chose not to request twelve legions of angels to protect Him from being unjustly arrested by a mob who eventually crucified Him, he showed mercy (Matt. 26:53).

When God met with Moses on Mount Sinai, He declared that He wants to be known as a God who shows goodness and truth, grace and mercy, and who is long-suffering.

> And the LORD descended in the cloud, and stood with him there, and proclaimed the name of the LORD. And the LORD passed by before him and proclaimed, "The LORD, the LORD God, merciful and gracious, longsuffering, and abundant in goodness and truth, keeping mercy for thousands, forgiving iniquity and transgression and sin, and that will by no means clear the guilty; visiting the iniquity of the fathers upon the children, and upon the children's children, unto the third and to the fourth generation." And Moses made haste, and bowed toward the earth, and worshipped. (Exod. 34:5–8 KJV)

Mercy is such a part of who God is that when He had a container made to hold the most precious and holy items belonging to His people (the ark of the covenant), He had a special lid made to cover the top of the ark.

> Make a mercy seat of pure gold. . . . Set the mercy seat on top of the ark and put the testimony that I will give you into the ark. I will meet with you there above the mercy seat, between the two cherubim that are over the ark of the testimony; I will speak with you from there about all that I command you regarding the Israelites. (Exod. 25:17, 21–22)

The place where God would come down to meet with His people was named the "mercy seat," comparable to the "throne of grace" spoken of in Hebrews 4:16. "Therefore let us come boldly unto the throne of grace, that we may obtain mercy, and find grace to help in time of need" (KJV). Showing mercy to others implies that you have the power to do otherwise, but choose instead to be merciful and forgive or not to hold a debtor's actions against them. God chose to provide us with a way to have our sins forgiven through repentance and faith in His Son. We, too, have the means by which we can forgive others when they sin against us and to release them from any obligation to us. Why does Christ command us to be merciful toward others? Because He was merciful toward us.

We read in the account of a Gentile named Cornelius that he was a merciful person. As Cornelius was praying, an angel appeared to Him. "Looking intently at him, he became afraid and said, 'What is it, lord?' The angel told him, 'Your prayers and your acts of charity have come up as a memorial offering before God'" (Acts 10:4). What we do in mercy toward others is stored up and presented to God Himself. God notices those who please Him. He rewards those who demonstrate His heart toward others. To be merciful is not only met with great relief to people but is building a monument of kindness before God.

Application: When was the last time you showed someone mercy? Was it to your husband or wife? Was it to your friend or your children? Was it to a relative or someone in the church or at work? Mercy is withholding a punishment, criticism, or rebuke that is rightfully deserved. Choosing to show mercy is choosing to care more for who the person is than what the person has done. This is pleasing to Christ.

5. Judge Not

- "Do not judge, and you will not be judged. Do not condemn, and you will not be condemned. Forgive, and you will be forgiven" (Luke 6:37; see Matt. 7:1).
- "Stop judging according to outward appearances; rather judge according to righteous judgment" (John 7:24).

Christ knows we have a propensity toward being judgmental. We can easily and quickly point out the failures and flaws of others and often more harshly than we would judge ourselves. The Bible tells us that Christ is the only Righteous Judge (2 Tim. 4:8). There are no others. There is no possible way for us to know everything about a person—their thoughts, their actions, their intentions, their circumstances, their motivations. But Christ does. We see only a person's actions, perhaps some of their omissions, and occasionally hear some of their thoughts. Yet what little we manage to put together we feel is adequate to pass judgment on them and then condemn them as guilty! The only way we can possibly come to a righteous judgment is if we can see a person's heart, and we cannot.

We are easily misled when we judge others by appearances. Appearances are deceiving at best. More often we see what we *want* to see rather than what truly is. David would never have been chosen king had the criterion been outward appearance. As Samuel examined his much larger and older brothers, God had something to say. "But the LORD said to Samuel, 'Do not look at his appearance or his stature, because I have rejected him. Man does not see what the LORD sees, for man sees what is visible, but the LORD sees the heart'" (1 Sam. 16:7).

Judging also puts us in a place of judgment *over* others and leads to pride, haughtiness, self-importance, and superiority—*none of which are characteristics of Christ.* It is easy to forget about our own flaws and shortcomings when we are busy pointing fingers at everyone else. However, there is an even more dangerous aspect of judging others.

- "Who are you to criticize another's household slave? Before his own Lord he stands or falls. And he will stand. For the Lord is able to make him stand" (Rom. 14:4).
- "Don't criticize one another, brothers. He who criticizes a brother or judges his brother criticizes the law and judges the law. But if you judge the law, you are not a doer of the law but a judge. There is one lawgiver and judge who is able to save and to destroy. But who are you to judge your neighbor?" (James 4:11–12).

Jesus recommends that before we start to pass judgment on others, we need to clean out our own closet and renovate our own lives so that we are pleasing to God. And that could take some time to do. Judgment starts at home, and when you begin to have an honest look at yourself, you will be able to look at others with the eyes of grace rather than looking down the long finger of criticism.

> "Why do you look at the speck in your brother's eye, but don't notice the log in your own eye? Or how can you say

> to your brother, 'Brother, let me take out the speck that is in your eye,' when you yourself don't see the log in your eye? Hypocrite! First take the log out of your eye, and then you will see clearly to take out the speck in your brother's eye." (Luke 6:41–42)

The danger is that when you judge or criticize others, you may be criticizing and judging their *Master and Lord* as well. Typically, we judge and criticize with limited information and often little relationship with the ones we are judging. When we get to know them, we can know their heart, their motivation, and find out where we may be able to help rather than simply pointing accusatory fingers at them from afar. Christ had every right to pass righteous judgment on us and find us guilty of capital offences, but instead He came down to become one of us, to love us, to walk with us, and to die in our place that we might live.

Application: Take time to get to know others before you give in to the temptation to judge them. Try to see Christ at work in them, or pray to that end, rather than condemning them or labeling them as not worthy of your time and efforts. Passing judgment will also quickly close the door to showing mercy and grace. Remember to "do unto others as you want them to do unto you."

6. Freely Give

- “Give to the one who asks you, and don’t turn away from the one who wants to borrow from you” (Matt. 5:42).
- “Give, and it will be given to you; a good measure—pressed down, shaken together, and running over—will be poured into your lap. For with the measure you use, it will be measured back to you” (Luke 6:38).
- “You have received free of charge; give free of charge” (Matt. 10:8).

You might get the impression from these verses that giving is important to Christ. It is. It is a major part of His nature and the Father’s nature to give. The Bible tells us (John 3:16) that God loved us so much that He *gave* us His One and Only Son to be the propitiation for our sins. There is nothing God is willing to withhold from us if it is in our best interest for Him to give it. In fact, Christ urges us to ask Him for what we need because He is already willing to give it to us. “I assure you: Anything you ask the Father in My name, He will give you” (John 16:23).

When we give, we show that our heart is in the right place. If we are reluctant to give, then we value what we possess more than we value our relationship with God. Holding tightly onto our possessions shows they have a tight hold on us. Christ wants us to be completely free from the trappings of this world so that nothing can be used against us, and nothing will command our loyalty more than Him.

- Would you be willing to sell your prized collector car that mostly sits covered in your garage if your church was in need of funds to build their building? Are you holding on to it, or is it holding on to you?
- Would you give your last twenty dollars to a single mom in need of groceries if it meant not going to that movie with your friends? Is your entertainment more important than her feeding her kids?

Christ gives us an interesting challenge in Matthew 5:40: "As for the one who wants to sue you and take away your shirt, let him have your coat as well." Wouldn't it shock your plaintiff if he needlessly sued you for five thousand dollars and you gave him *six* thousand dollars? Or if your neighbor demanded that you fix a scratch on his car door made by your child and you had his entire car repainted and cleaned instead? Generosity and giving show that you are the master over your possessions and that they do not control you.

Giving shows we can hold on to our things loosely, as stewards of what God has given us. We can give to others in need knowing it is pleasing to God and it is good for our own heart. It also develops good character in children who need to see their parents being generous to others. Do you have a habit of dropping coins into the hat of those living on the street (remember: don't judge others)? To Christ, giving is not optional; it is a demonstration of our gratitude to Him when we help those in need. Jesus explains,

"The one who has two shirts must share with someone who has none, and the one who has food must do the same" (Luke 3:11).

Do you remember what happened to one of the greediest persons in Jericho when Christ encountered his life? When Christ entered his home and entered his life, his priorities changed. Zacchaeus's actions demonstrated his gratefulness to his Lord. "But Zacchaeus stood there and said to the Lord, 'Look, I'll give half of my possessions to the poor, Lord! And if I have extorted anything from anyone, I'll pay back four times as much!'" (Luke 19:8).

Giving is not so much a character issue as it is a lordship issue. Whoever or whatever controls your life is your Lord and Master. Matthew, Mark, and Luke record an incident where a rich man came to Jesus looking for eternal life. He had kept all the commandments yet still felt something was missing. "Then, looking at him, Jesus loved him and said to him, 'You lack one thing. Go, sell all you have and give to the poor, and you will have treasure in heaven. Then come, follow Me.' But he was stunned at this demand, and he went away grieving, because he had many possessions" (Mark 10:21–22). In the giving away of his possessions, this rich man had trouble. He was not willing to let go in order to hold on to Christ.

Let me assure you, one visit to an orphanage in Russia; to a rural elementary school in Senegal, West Africa; or to a small village in India will help put things into perspective. A wise man once said to me, "If you have anything in your home whose sole purpose is to collect dust, you have more than 80 percent of people in the world." Giving helps keep our heart in check and our loyalties where they belong.

- "Remember this: the person who sows sparingly will also reap sparingly, and the person who sows generously will also reap generously" (2 Cor. 9:6).
- "Each person should do as he has decided in his heart—not reluctantly or out of necessity, for God loves a cheerful giver" (2 Cor. 9:7).

Application: Do you really have to keep up with your neighbors or spend so much money on gifts at Christmas? Do you really have to have the latest electronics when the old version you have still works fine? Consider for a moment if your house was burning uncontrollably. What would you try to save? Your photo albums? Your coin collection? Your documents? Your enormous flat screen TV or surround system? Remember, where you heart is, there your treasure is also. If you do not treasure the Lord above all, and His kingdom next, you may need to ask Him to help you straighten out your priorities.

7. Be Perfect

- "Be perfect, therefore, as your heavenly Father is perfect" (Matt. 5:48).

This command comes at the end of one of Christ's most notable teachings, that of the Sermon on the Mount. In this chapter Christ covers a lot of ground. He speaks of the character and nature that He looks for in His followers, that they be humble, meek, merciful, peacemakers, and willing to turn the other cheek in the midst of adversity. He speaks of the traditional expectations for God's people, then places His own expectations on top in a series of teachings beginning with, "You have heard it said . . . ," then adds, "But I say to you. . . ." He takes what people had thought was good enough in their own eyes and raises the expectations much higher to that which is good enough in God's eyes. Then He concludes this chapter with, "Be perfect, therefore, as your heavenly Father is perfect" (Matt. 5:48).

This may be a reflection of what Moses wrote, "Thou shalt be perfect with the LORD thy God" (Deut. 18:13 KJV). What is meant here is not that we are to have the same degree of perfection in love, righteousness, justice, grace, or other characteristics of God as He has. But we must imitate Him as closely as humanly possible. We are to walk uprightly and with sincerity before Him. We are to do all we can to represent Him to others as accurately as a man or woman can do. We are to live lives that reflect His heart, His justice, His righteousness, His love, and His values before a watching world and before God Himself so that we bring glory to Him. To be perfect is to have the same type of relationship with God and before God as Christ had.

This command does not reflect the commonly held mantra, "Do everything with excellence," as if that were pleasing to God. God alone is excellent. Nothing we *do* is excellent in His sight. Our feeble attempts at excellence seem more to impress visitors in our congregation than to please God. No, God wants *perfection.* He demands holiness and righteousness. *Excellence* is an outward attempt to impress God that often seems more to impress others who can't compete. Holiness, righteousness, and perfection are designed to please God, which all come not from what we *do* but from who we *are.*

Look at the scene below when the prophet Azariah helped King Asa and the people become right with God:

> They were gathered in Jerusalem. . . . At that time they sacrificed to the LORD 700 cattle and 7,000 sheep from all the plunder they had brought. Then they entered into a covenant to seek the LORD God of their ancestors with all their mind and all their heart. Whoever would not seek the LORD God of Israel would be put to death, young or old, man or woman. They took an oath to the LORD in a loud voice, with shouting, with trumpets, and with rams' horns. All Judah rejoiced over the oath, for they had sworn it with all their mind. They had sought Him with all their

> heart, and He was found by them. So the LORD gave them rest on every side. (2 Chron. 15:10–15)

God revealed Himself to His people and rewarded them with rest from war only after they sought Him "with all their mind and all their heart." It was not the quality of their sound system that impressed God or the beautiful harmonies of their choirs. He did not tip His hat at the wonderful oratory of the day's speaker or give a nod to the inspiring dramatic presentation or video clip. It doesn't even proclaim His pleasure with the seventy-seven hundred animals that were sacrificed. He looked to their hearts. He saw their enthusiasm and yearning to seek Him with their whole desire. "For I desire loyalty and not sacrifice, the knowledge of God rather than burnt offerings" (Hos. 6:6). It requires less to give offerings and gifts to God than it does to give our hearts to Him and to make the necessary changes to be like Him.

God prefers one person who truly and passionately seeks Him over a thousand slick, excellent, motivating, perfectly timed, and television-ready worship services. The only way to achieve perfection in the eyes of God is to have a heart that truly, unashamedly, passionately, and wholly seeks after Him.

Application: If you have been presenting God something that you *do* rather than being the person He wants you to *be* in your heart, repent, ask Him for forgiveness, and take care of your heart before you present Him your activity. Do you aspire to be perfect, or have you given up, considering it an unattainable goal? Ask His Spirit to guide you into a perfect relationship with your heavenly Father.

8. Don't Be a Hypocrite

- "Whenever you pray, you must not be like the hypocrites" (Matt. 6:5).
- "Whenever you fast, don't be sad-faced like the hypocrites" (Matt. 6:16).

A hypocrite does not actually believe what he is saying to others because his actions reveal the opposite. Here Christ points out not just the hypocrisy of the religious leaders but all those who had bought into their pious and misdirected religious activity that was for show rather than for God. In His rebuke, Christ affirms the need for prayer and its benefits. Likewise, Christ affirms the practice of fasting or the denial of food for the sake of seeking God. Both were legitimate and valuable activities that were being misused and abused by those who should have known better.

Both prayer and fasting were meant to draw oneself closer to God, but the religious hypocrites were using it as a means of drawing attention to themselves—not God's attention, but people's attention. What they did was for show. What was meant for devotion, humility, and dedication to God was turned into a farcical activity that actually dishonored God and brought condemnation upon the individual.

His rebuke of this hypocrisy also has its attending corrective instructions on what God is looking for in prayer and fasting.

Both prayer and fasting were designed to help individuals come to the place where their lives were right before God, and in this state God would be able to speak with them and give them the guidance they sought. To use prayer as a means to enhance one's reputation among people was an abuse of a privilege and an affront to God. Jesus admonishes us to use our time in prayer and fasting as a private, focused activity, free from distractions, where one's heart and mind can be clearly centered on God for extended periods of time. When we truly seek God first, He then is able to reward us with the very thing the hypocrites were seeking all along. "Your Father who sees in secret will reward you" (Matt. 6:18).

When our Father rewards us openly, we will get a certain amount of attention from others who will want to know why we are so blessed by God. But to seek the attention first without any intention of truly seeking God is not only a waste of our time but a demonstration that we have given our hearts over to other gods and actually forsaken the God we purport to worship.

Application: Some people refuse to pray in public; that is not what this is talking about. God's children can all come before their heavenly Father and call on His name together. The question is, to whom are you actually talking when you pray with others? If your words are meant to impress those around you, then they do not impress God. If your prayers flow out of your intimate relationship with God, others will be moved in their spirit to agree with you in their hearts. Prayer is meant to interact with God, not to manipulate or impress those around you.

9. Don't Swear an Oath—Have Integrity

- "Again, you have heard that it was said to our ancestors, You must not break your oath, but you must keep your oaths to the Lord. But I tell you, don't take an oath at all: either by heaven, because it is God's throne; or by the earth, because it is His footstool; or by Jerusalem, because it is the city of the great King. Neither should you swear by your head, because you cannot make a single hair white or black. But let your word 'yes,' be 'yes,' and your 'no' be 'no.' Anything more than this is from the evil one" (Matt. 5:33–37).

Here we must distinguish between "cursing" and "taking oaths." This passage is referring to making an "oath" for the sake of adding weight to the promises you have made. We are not as familiar with this in the Western world; instead we like to use written and verbal contracts that outline what our obligation is and what the penalty is if we do not fulfill our obligation. The point of this command is to be a person of your word. We should never need to ask God to strike us dead, to swear by the heavens, or "as God is my witness," or swear on our "mother's grave," or on the "head of my saintly aunt" when making a promise, none of which makes any sense in the first place. Our daily lives need to be lived in such a way that our character and reputation is a good enough bond. Anyone who needs to swear by things they have no control over has a problem with their character. It means that they are not trustworthy or their reputation has preceded them, which apparently is not a good thing.

Every promise of God was fulfilled. Every commitment of Christ was completely satisfied. "For every one of God's promises is 'Yes' in Him. Therefore the 'Amen' is also spoken through Him by us for God's glory" (2 Cor. 1:20). No one can bring just accusation against the character of God or His Son because they both have acted righteously in all things and there is no question that what they say will come about. This command reflects the contemporary phrase, "My word is my bond," which means "my word is my guarantee or pledge," and that should be good enough. Others may need contracts or written guarantees, but those who deal with Christians should be able to count on them at all times to fulfill their obligations and that which was promised.

Application: Do you know what your reputation is? Are you trustworthy? Do people count on you to come through for them? Are you a person of your word? If not, you are not representing Christ very well, and you are giving Christians a bad name. People are watching you, and you are either building up the name of Christ in being faithful and trustworthy, or you are bringing disgrace on His name by being negligent and of poor character. Let your word be worth gold.

4

Concerning Others

Let your light shine before men, so that they may see your good works and give glory to your Father in heaven.

Matthew 5:16

Christ's love for people is consistently reflected in His commands. *We* are not the focus of Christ's attention and affections; *everyone* is. If we think the commands of Christ are primarily designed for our own character development and benefit, we are mistaken. That is only half of it. They are also designed so that as our lives reflect Christ more and more, we will draw people into Christ's presence. When people see how we live and how we treat others, they should be able to see Christ in action. Christ wants us to treat others as He would treat them because only then can we truly represent Him to others. If we do not genuinely demonstrate His love to those around us, we will endanger our ability to relate to God.

God has always connected our relationships toward those around us with our relationship to Him. He cares how we treat the orphans, the widows, and the strangers in our midst as well as our brothers and sisters in Christ. As Christians we function in community, not in isolation. We are a part of *His* kingdom, not ours; and it is a daily honor and privilege to be Christ's ambassadors to the world. Letting our light shine is an obvious, outward activity that will draw attention to ourselves and to Christ who resides in us, the result of which will be that others will give glory to God, not to us. If we receive the glory, the honor, and the praise for our many good works, then something is dreadfully wrong in what we are doing, or at least in the way we are doing it. May we honor Him in our thoughts and words as well as our deeds so that others will see Christ in us and give Him all the glory.

1. Love One Another

- "This is what I command you: Love one another" (John 15:17).
- "This is My command: Love one another as I have loved you" (John 15:12).
- "I give you a new command: Love one another. Just as I have loved you, you must also love one another. By this all people will know that you are My disciples, if you have love for one another" (John 13:34–35).

This command can be seen as a summary of all Christ's commands, an aerial view at the purpose behind the commands. It is as though Christ's commands have a single purpose in mind, or an overall goal that they are trying to achieve in our life focus, our character, our perspectives, and our life's work for Him. Love has always been a central theme that permeates all of God's activity both in the Old Testament as He related to His people and in the New Testament as He reveals Himself through His Son Jesus Christ. John 14–17 is heavily laden with significant truths and valuable assurances from Christ for His people. The word "love" is found no fewer than twenty-eight times in John 13–17. As these were some of the final words of Christ prior to His being arrested, they carry great significance as Christ wanted to impress them on His disciples.

Christ had to *command* His people to love one another. One would think love would naturally pour out of His people from simple gratitude and gratefulness for all God has done for us. I suppose this should not be a surprise though, if Paul also had to command husbands to love their wives (Eph. 5:28, 33) and encourage wives to love their husbands and their children (Titus 2:4)! We must work to perfect our love.

Christ says the telltale sign of a true disciple is if he has love for his fellow Christians. The standard for what that type of love looks like was demonstrated by the One who gave the command. There could have been so many other criteria for determining that a person was a genuine follower of Christ, but the One who is love wanted us to demonstrate His love to others in a public and obvious way. This love was meant to be seen by believers and nonbelievers alike and would serve as a means to draw people to Christ's love through us. Unfortunately, we tend to water down this command to mean we are to be *nice* to one another or be *polite* to one another or not to harm others. If we fail this test of love toward one another, then we also fail in our love for Christ. "If anyone says, 'I love God,' yet hates his brother, he is a liar. For the person who does not love his brother he has seen cannot love the God he has not seen" (1 John 4:20).

Although this command seems fairly straightforward, it is for several reasons one of the most difficult to follow of all Christ's commands.

First, in order to love others, we must continually fight against our tendency toward selfishness and self-centeredness. This was evident from the garden of Eden onward.

Second, we have terribly distorted God's definition of love to become such things as lust, control, manipulation, greed, addiction, infatuation, obsession, and passion—all of which fall short of true love. This is why Christ did not just *tell* us about love; He *showed* us what love looked like so we would have no question or doubt in our minds.

Third, we tend not to make the connection between our actions toward others and our love toward God. In fact, I doubt seriously that we truly and completely understand how to love God with all of our heart, all of our soul, all of our strength, and all of our mind. Many seek to serve Him, please Him, honor Him, or worship Him; but loving someone we have not seen is challenging, perhaps even mysterious. If we truly understood how to love God fully, we would not have any significant problems with loving one another.

Of course the ultimate act of love was demonstrated by Christ on the cross.

- "No one has greater love than this, that someone would lay down his life for his friends. You are My friends if you do what I command you" (John 15:13–14).

It is sobering to realize that this is exactly the kind of love Christ expects His followers to demonstrate for one another. Most would be willing to give their life to save a child or a spouse, even perhaps a dear friend or relative. But to give one's life for strangers and enemies is showing a level of love I think we can scarcely comprehend.

Application: Can you truly say you love others? Can you truly say you love God? Some people respect God, some fear Him, some admire Him, or seek to please Him. But they have trouble loving

Him. It is easier to love others when we understand we are actually letting Christ love them through us. When Christ said, "I assure you: Whoever receives anyone I send receives Me, and the one who receives Me receives Him who sent Me" (John 13:20), He meant that loving others is, in effect, loving Christ. We don't love others because they deserve to be loved; we love them because we owe it to Christ to love them. The only way we can truly love others with genuine, authentic, Christlike love is to allow Christ's love for others to flow through us. When we are able to love others truly and selflessly, we begin to understand the heart of God Himself. Accepting His love is far more than an emotion, and it always leads to action that helps us go the next step in loving others.

2. Love Your Enemies

- "But I say to you who listen: Love your enemies, do what is good to those who hate you, bless those who curse you, pray for those who mistreat you" (Luke 6:27–28).

This command goes against our natural tendencies. We prefer to get even, to seek justice, to stand up for our rights, or to defend our honor or reputation. But to show love to our enemies challenges us at our core. In some ways it is a test of our resolve as believers, and it reveals the level of commitment we have for Christ. We show love to our enemies not because we actually and genuinely love them but because we actually and genuinely love Christ. But in loving our enemies and doing good to those who hate us, we see the potential for our enemies to become our brothers and sisters in Christ.

As Paul and Silas languished in the Philippian jail, their "enemy," the chief jailor, stood guard over them. As the Lord used an earthquake to open the prison doors, Paul cried out to the jailor to put away his sword and not to take his own life. Paul's love for Christ allowed him to show love for his enemy, and that night one who had done great physical harm to God's servants became a servant of God and a brother in Christ.

Application: Christ's goal is not to make our lives more comfortable or prosperous; His primary goal is to redeem the lost before they enter into eternity without Him. Loving our enemies is a major part of that plan. If we are unable to love our enemies, we are not fully able to love Christ either. Will you choose four people you have the most trouble liking and pray for them today? Will you send them notes of encouragement? Will you do something this week that proves to them you are a follower of Christ?

3. Turn the Other Cheek

- "If anyone hits you on the cheek, offer the other also. And if anyone takes away your coat, don't hold back your shirt either. Give to everyone who asks from you, and from one who takes away your things, don't ask for them back" (Luke 6:29–30).

How important are your belongings to you? Your books, your power tools, your camping gear, your tennis racquet, your car equipment and accessories? Are they more important than your relationships with people? Are they more important than having an opportunity to share the gospel with a lost person?

This command hits at the issue of your priorities and how they may conflict with the priorities of Christ. Christ was unencumbered with stuff. He did not have a car or boat to maintain, nor did He have an art collection or cabin at the lake. I don't think He had a wheelbarrow or shovel once He began His ministry. He had absolutely nothing to distract Him from His purpose on the earth. There was nothing to compete for His attention, nothing to waste His time, nothing with which to fritter away the hours in solitude. People and His relationship with His Father were the only two things that mattered to Him. Every time we add another collectible or tool, or upgrade our many other items we store in our garage, we take time away from eternal matters. We must hold onto our things loosely and never allow them to become more important to us than the people around us. Whatever we have should be used for eternal purposes rather than personal, private pleasures.

Do you still resent that person who broke something of yours, or who never returned your book, or who inadvertently scratched your car? If you do, you love your things more than you love people. We can call it good stewardship, taking care of our investment, or a host of other things; but what do you think Christ would call it? How many of your things would be impressive to Him? I wonder how many more people could be reached with the gospel if the money spent on collectibles, trinkets, unnecessary upgrades, and toys was used in mission work around the world. We can't take any of it with us, and much of what we leave behind will be sold off, thrown out, or stored away by those we leave it to. The goal for the Christian is not worldly investments but kingdom investments. We store in heaven all that is truly important, and it waits for us to finish our time on the earth.

- "As for the one who wants to sue you and take away your shirt, let him have your coat as well. And if anyone forces you to go one mile, go with him two" (Matt. 5:40–41).
- "Reach a settlement quickly with your adversary while you're on the way with him, or your adversary will hand you over to the judge, the judge to the officer, and you will be thrown into prison" (Matt. 5:25).

Some things are more important than our comfort or convenience. We are ambassadors for Christ (2 Cor. 5:20) and represent Him at all times. This will often require us to be inconvenienced, to sacrifice our time or resources, or to face the wrath of others who are enemies to Christ.

We are each individuals doing our part in a much grander plan of which Christ is the architect. Giving in to the demands of others for the sake of Christ, settling differences quickly for the sake of Christ, and sacrificing our resources for the sake of Christ will not go unnoticed by Christ who rewards His faithful ones accordingly. No, we are not to be doormats or slaves to the whims of others, but we are to be servants of Christ, who should be quick to volunteer when Christ gives an assignment. We are not to be needlessly walked over or abused by our enemies or constantly cheated by selfish and arrogant people; instead we are to die to self, take up our cross daily, and follow Him where He leads us. We are not the slaves of others but the servants of Christ. There is a significant difference.

Application: There is sometimes a fine line between being good stewards of our possessions and our possessions being stewards of us. If you have anything that takes more of your time than you give to ministering to people, your possessions are far too high on your priority list. Would you have trouble leaving everything behind and following Christ today? Dusting collectibles, polishing a shiny boat or car, retuning that engine to get it perfect, or making room for yet another piece of art for your wall are likely not as worthwhile to Christ as they are to you. Everything has its place, but do your things have their right place in your life? Are you spending more time plotting to get even with someone who has hurt you than you do praying for them? Have you thought about how to make your enemy your brother or sister in Christ?

4. Forgive

- "Be on your guard. If your brother sins, rebuke him, and if he repents, forgive him. And if he sins against you seven times in a day and comes back to you seven times, saying, 'I repent,' you must forgive him" (Luke 17:3–4).

Forgiveness is another important part of God's nature, and it is not surprising that Christ requires it of us. We cannot strive to be Christlike without also learning to forgive as He did. Right to the end, even while nailed upon the cross, some of His last words were, "Father, forgive them, because they do not know what they are doing" (Luke 23:34). Christ knows forgiveness can set us free from rage, bitterness, pride, and hatred toward others. As long as we refuse to forgive others, we are in bondage, and we are refusing to let God use us in any significant way in the life of that person. "Then Peter came to Him and said, 'Lord, how many times could my brother sin against me and I forgive him? As many as seven times?' 'I tell you, not as many as seven,' Jesus said to him, 'but 70 times seven'" (Matt. 18:21–22).

Unforgiveness allows the root of bitterness (Heb. 12:15) to grow in our hearts and minds and prevent us from pursuing peace and holiness (Heb. 12:14). Paul reminds us that Christ entrusted us with a special ministry, a ministry of reconciliation; and as Christ's ambassadors, we are able to help facilitate the reconciling of people with God. As long as we are at odds with people and carry unforgiveness in our hearts, we are not at peace with God, and we cannot help others find God either.

> Everything is from God, who reconciled us to Himself through Christ and gave us the ministry of reconciliation: That is, in Christ, God was reconciling the world to Himself, not counting their trespasses against them, and He has committed the message of reconciliation to us. Therefore, we are ambassadors for Christ; certain that God is appealing through us, we plead on Christ's behalf, "Be reconciled to God." (2 Cor. 5:18–20)

Another aspect of forgiveness is perhaps even more serious. In Christ's model prayer He says, "And forgive us our debts, as we also have forgiven our debtors. . . . For if you forgive people their wrongdoing, your heavenly Father will forgive you as well. But if you don't forgive people, your Father will not forgive your wrongdoing" (Matt. 6:12, 14–15). And in Mark 11:25 Jesus instructs us, "And whenever you stand praying, if you have anything against anyone, forgive him, so that your Father in heaven will also forgive you your wrongdoing."

The sense here is that we have the ability to prevent God's forgiveness of our own sins if we refuse to forgive those who have sinned against us. This is not an easy concept to understand. We were forgiven when we gave our lives over to Christ, but our subsequent sinning can still cause barriers in our relationship to God. When we carry sin in our hearts, the Spirit is not free to accomplish His will in us because we are holding on to things that are offensive to God. When we forgive others, we also remove the barriers so the Spirit can work in our own hearts and lives.

Application: You may have painful memories in your past or scars that you carry with you from past relationships or situations. Ask God now to help you let these things go, to help you release them into His hands and take care of them in His way. Ask Him to give you freedom from the bondage in which they have kept you these long years. Forgive and you will feel the wave of freedom wash over you as the Spirit refreshes your soul with His presence. Forgive and you will release the Spirit to be at home in your heart and not be impeded by the bitterness and unforgiveness that clutters your heart. Forgive so you can be at peace and not let anything prevent you from ministering to those to whom God has placed in your pathway.

5. Go and Be Reconciled with Others

- "So if you are offering your gift on the altar, and there you remember that your brother has something against you, leave your gift there in front of the altar. First go and be reconciled with your brother, and then come and offer your gift" (Matt. 5:23–24).

This command shows that God prefers *reconciliation* over *worship*. In fact, our worship, our praise, our tithes, and our songs are not acceptable to God until we are reconciled with our brother or sister in Christ. This reflects the apostle John's later writings, where he tells us, "If anyone says, 'I love God,' yet hates his brother, he is a liar. For the person who does not love his brother he has seen cannot love the God he has not seen" (1 John 4:20). To say we love God and want to worship Him while maintaining unresolved issues with one of His children is impossible. We show our love to God by loving His people and treating them as He would treat them. To allow an issue to be unresolved between us and others shows contempt for God and His desire for us to be at peace with one another.

Notice this verse does not say, "If you remember *you* have something against your brother"; it says, "If you remember your brother has something against *you*." It should always be our aim to be at peace with one another among God's family in particular and with those in the outside community in general. Of course this is not always possible, but as far as it concerns you, you are to make every effort to be at peace with all men, to go the extra mile, to make the extra effort because of your love for God.

Paul writes:

- "Pursue peace with everyone, and holiness—without it no one will see the Lord" (Heb. 12:14).
- "So then, we must pursue what promotes peace and what builds up one another" (Rom. 14:19).
- "If possible, on your part, live at peace with everyone" (Rom. 12:18).

We cannot go merrily into His presence ignoring the fact that we have hurt those He loves. Imagine trying to gain favor with a father after you have needlessly harmed his child. Reparations must be made and relationships restored before we come before our Father if we have hurt one of *His* children.

The pursuit of peace is a worthy goal for the believer! Over and over the New Testament describes God as a God of peace (Rom. 15:33; 16:20; 1 Cor. 14:33; Phil. 4:7; 1 Thess. 5:23). He wants to see His people living at peace with one another. It is simply unacceptable for us to ignore our responsibility to our fellow man while we attempt to give our lives to God for His service. God looks to the heart, not the lips. Our actions speak louder than our words. If we are not actively promoting peace, building up one another, and doing everything in our power to repair broken relationships, we will find our worship empty and cold, and God very quiet indeed.

Application: Do you have outstanding issues with anyone? Does anyone have an outstanding issue with you? God will not allow you to pretend to worship Him if you are not making the effort to be reconciled with others. Is there a phone call or a letter you need to write before your next worship service so that your worship will be acceptable to God? Take a moment to reflect on your relationships with others. Are there those you have offended inadvertently or deliberately, or those you know who have not forgiven you for some offense and still hold grudges against you? The Scriptures say, "If possible, on your part, live at peace with everyone," which means you must go the extra mile, make the extra effort, do what others would say is above and beyond the call of duty to reconcile with them. The purpose of this command is not only to demonstrate love but also to remove anything that could prevent experiencing the full meaning of worship toward God. Make a conscious effort with your spouse, children, close friends, or family to ask them specifically if you have done anything that has offended them, and beg their forgiveness if there is. Unfulfilled promises, inadvertent remarks, unjustified criticism, impatience, anger, and pride can leave scars on others. Make it right as soon as possible.

6. Treat Others as You Want to Be Treated

- "'Which of these three do you think proved to be a neighbor to the man who fell into the hands of the robbers?' 'The one who showed mercy to him,' he said. Then Jesus told him, 'Go and do the same'" (Luke 10:36–37).
- "Just as you want others to do for you, do the same for them" (Luke 6:31).

The story of the good Samaritan shows more of Christ's expectations for His people. He commands us to "go and do the same." To treat others in the same way we wish to be treated. To love our neighbor as we love ourself. Love always requires action of some kind. It goes beyond feelings and emotions and causes us to get involved in the lives of hurting people all around us. To turn a blind eye, to walk on the other side of the road, means we have done the same to Christ. "And the King will answer them, 'I assure you: Whatever you did for one of the least of these brothers of Mine, you did for Me'" (Matt. 25:40).

We are to show mercy just as Christ has shown it to us. We are to forgive others in the same way Christ forgave us. We are to love others as Christ has loved us. We are to go the extra mile just as Christ has done with us on so many occasions. "For I have given you an example," Jesus says, "that you also should do just as I have done for you" (John 13:15). Treating others as we want to be treated is doing what Christ would have done for them had He been in the same situation. He cares for those He has created, and He loves each one dearly. Too many people wait for others to act kindly toward them and never get around to demonstrating kindness toward others. Don't be one of those people!

Application: The next time you see a person in need and get the urge to do something about it, *do it* instead of just thinking about it. Put your urge into action and make a difference in Jesus' name. Think of what you appreciate others doing for you the most, and plan this week to do that for someone else. Random acts of kindness often have more impact than you could ever imagine. Let God guide you to be a positive and encouraging influence on those around you, and watch the difference it will make in your relationship with them.

5

Calling

Therefore, brothers, make every effort to confirm your calling and election, because if you do these things you will never stumble.

2 Peter 1:10

A calling is personal, humbling, and intentional. It is initiated and instituted by God and not requested or sought out by those who desire it. We do not take out a membership in God's kingdom that is renewed annually, nor do we sign up to be on His "team." We are *called* by God Himself, we are *chosen* by the King of kings, and we are *selected* by our Creator, even *conscripted* into a love relationship with Jesus Christ Himself. When we answer or accept that call, we enter into an unusual and divine relationship with our Lord. We are no longer our own; we were purchased with a costly price (1 Cor. 7:23; Acts 20:28).

The fact that we no longer belong to ourselves but to the One who called us is significant. Not only does this identify to whom we belong and place us in God's kingdom, but we are also now identifiable to the enemies of Christ as companion targets for attack. Realizing we are secure in our calling as long as we abide in Christ gives us great comfort. But we must be aware of our vulnerability to temptation and to attack as God's chosen ones. "For our battle is not against flesh and blood, but against the rulers, against the authorities, against the world powers of this darkness, against the spiritual forces of evil in the heavens" (Eph. 6:12).

We have been *called* by God, and we have been *commissioned* by our Lord to go and continue His ministry while we remain on the earth. Christ was physically limited to what an individual could do while in human form. But as Spirit, Christ is now able to work through every individual in which He has taken up residence (John 14:23). As Paul said, "For me, living is Christ" (Phil. 1:21). Peter also reminds us, "For you were called to this, because Christ also suffered for you, leaving you an example, so that you should follow in His steps" (1 Pet. 2:21). We can make our calling sure by abiding in Christ and letting Him live through us each and every day, bringing glory and honor to the Father through us. What an exciting relationship we have with God and our Lord Jesus Christ!

1. Seek First God's Kingdom

- "But seek first the kingdom of God and His righteousness, and all these things will be provided for you" (Matt. 6:33).
- "Don't collect for yourselves treasures on earth, where moth and rust destroy and where thieves break in and steal. But collect for yourselves treasures in heaven, where neither moth nor rust destroys, and where thieves don't break in and steal. For where your treasure is, there your heart will be also" (Matt. 6:19–21).

Everyone has values and priorities in their life. You can look at a person's bank account statement to discover what many of these priorities are. The Bible tells us, "For where your treasure is, there your heart will be also" (Matt. 6:21). You use your time, money, energy, creative thinking, and resources on your priority items. If you value sports, you likely will spend time playing them, buying electronic sports games, collecting sports cards, watching sports on TV, reading sports magazines, buying tickets to sports games, monitoring game results on the Internet, and purchasing sports merchandise and more. If you value family, you will spend your money and time on family activities, great family vacations, attending parent meetings, going to your kid's games and performances, buying toys and equipment for your family to use, and more. If you value electronics, you will spend time studying them, fixing them, buying them, repairing them, comparing them, and upgrading them. The same goes for gardens, cars, collections, rock climbing, etc. We all have things that interest us and that draw our time and attention and money into them.

Christ wants us to put first things first and make sure the vast majority of our thoughts, actions, energy, and time is spent on what is truly important and what will truly last. If we neglect what is eternal for what is temporary, our treasure is based on misplaced values. Christ promises to give us everything we need once we have our heart in the right place. But when we chase after the things we *think* we need instead of focusing on kingdom matters, we assume responsibility for what Christ promised to do for us. Christ doesn't provide those things we are already providing for ourselves. We can focus on immediate pleasure, which leads to eternal consequences. But when we seek first the eternal kingdom, we receive so much more in the here and now than we had ever known was possible.

Wouldn't you rather have your needs supplied by the Lord than to try to manage all those details yourself? He provides your job, home, friends, support, health, safety, and a myriad of blessings when you honor Him first in your life. King Solomon learned this truth, telling us to "trust in the Lord with all your heart, and do not rely on your own understanding; think about Him in all your ways, and He will guide you on the right paths" (Prov. 3:5–6). Then in almost the same breath, he instructed his young reader to "honor the Lord with your possessions and with the first produce of your entire harvest; then your barns will be completely filled, and your vats will overflow with new wine" (Prov. 3:9–10). Putting everything in God's hands is the path to joy and provision.

Application: Do you trust God to supply *all* your needs or just the ones you can't manage on your own? Have you ever given Him the chance? If you have been spending all your time in *your* work taking care of *your* own needs, then you have not been spending much time in *His* work. His work is eternal; your work is temporary. His kingdom will last forever; yours will be gone in the blink of an eye. Seek His kingdom first, and let Him take care of yours along the way. You will be shocked at what God does in your own life as you invest in His work. When you work, work as unto the Lord. When you play, remember that the time you invest there also belongs to the Lord. Use all of your time wisely so when you might give an account to the Lord on judgment day, you will have nothing that will cause you shame.

2. Go . . . Baptize . . . Teach

- "Then Jesus came near and said to them, 'All authority has been given to Me in heaven and on earth. Go, therefore, and make disciples of all nations, baptizing them in the name of the Father and of the Son and of the Holy Spirit, teaching them to observe everything I have commanded you. And remember, I am with you always, to the end of the age'" (Matt. 28:18–20).
- "Then He said to them, 'Go into all the world and preach the gospel to the whole creation. Whoever believes and is baptized will be saved, but whoever does not believe will be condemned'" (Mark 16:15–16).

These two commands were some of the last Christ gave before ascending to heaven following His resurrection. They were designed for the purpose of helping His followers know without question what their life priorities should be until His return. If you follow the previous command, you should never have to worry about how to spend your time or how to use your spiritual gifts or where to invest your money and resources. In whatever we do, there should always be an awareness that we have been commanded to help the lost become found, bring hope to the hopeless, and do whatever we can to snatch people from the kingdom of darkness and bring them with us into the kingdom of light. These commands continue Christ's work on earth through His people as they obey Him.

Matthew 28:18–20 is often called the "Great Commission." A commission is an assignment, a task, or an office given by a higher authority. When a commission is accepted, it becomes one's purpose in life, and their priorities are reoriented to fulfill the obligation of the commission until it is completed. Truthfully, Christ's commission will likely not be fulfilled in our lifetime, so Christians do what they can where they have been placed until they are relieved of their commission by the One who gave it.

As we go and make disciples for Christ, we are to baptize them and teach them and help them understand that they, too, have been given a commission by Christ. The job is not done after we have made disciples; we must complete the task by helping them come to maturity in Christ, which means they are also to replicate the commission in their own lives.

Keep in mind this was not merely a good suggestion, a thought to consider, or a choice of various tasks to partake in when we have nothing better to do. Neither is it unreasonable, overbearing, or demanding; but it is incredibly important. If we ignore it, the result will be eternally devastating for those God has placed around us who do not yet know Him personally.

Many of Christ's commands are for our own personal growth and development as Christians, but this one moves beyond ourselves to our family members, our colleagues at work, our acquaintances at the ball field, and our neighbors who surround our homes. This command is an expansion, or an application of the second Great Commandment, to love our neighbor as ourself. As we worship God in our church, our neighbors need to worship God as well. As we serve the Lord, our neighbors also need to serve the Lord. As we have confidence that we will be taken up to heaven when Christ returns, they, too, need such confidence for their lives. We have this assurance for our souls, and it is our privilege and honor to be able to help them become brothers and sisters in Christ and experience the same assurance for their souls.

Application: With whom have you shared the gospel lately? With whom have you shared your testimony of how you came to Christ and what He has done in your life? Do several people come to mind when asked whom you have led to Christ? What reason could you possibly give Christ for not sharing the gospel if He came to visit you today? Sharing the gospel and making disciples is something that should come naturally to every believer in Christ. Telling others about Jesus should overflow from the joy you have within you. If you are one of those who rarely, if ever, shares your faith in Christ with others, you may want to consider afresh what eternity apart from Christ will mean for those around you. Ask God's Spirit to give you both the courage and the words to say; then just open your mouth and tell your friends about the Person who is most important to you in your life and how He helps you, guides you, and carries you in difficult times. Pray now for those around you that you know are lost, and ask God to give you opportunities each day to be a faithful witness to the transforming power of Christ in your life.

3. Go into All the World

- "Go into all the world and preach the gospel to the whole creation" (Mark 16:15).
- "Go, therefore, and make disciples of all nations, baptizing them in the name of the Father and of the Son and of the Holy Spirit, teaching them to observe everything I have commanded you" (Matt. 28:19–20).

This can be one of the most challenging commands to understand and implement, for it can require a great deal of determined focus and personal sacrifice. It was given to all of Christ's followers, not just those with valid passports. Most Christians prefer to send *others* into "all the world" and stay home to pray for them and perhaps support them financially rather than go themselves.

For a host of reasons people are unable to go to a foreign country and share the gospel with those who have not heard it. People say they cannot afford to travel, or they cannot get time off work, or they have dependents at home to care for, or they are afraid to fly, or they have special diets they have to maintain, or they don't feel safe. The list is endless as to why people feel they are unable to obey this command. To compensate, people give a few dollars to missionaries to assuage their guilt. Still Christ says, "Go"; make every effort to do everything possible to share the gospel with anyone anywhere who needs to hear it.

Yes, our mission field is our family, our neighborhood, our city, our state/province, our nation, but look again at this command. We are to go into "all the world"; we are to "teach all nations." We are to do our utmost to give every single person on the earth the opportunity to accept Christ as Savior and Lord. Christian Web sites have seen over a million people around the world saved. Many businessmen who travel to numerous countries go as much as Christ's ambassadors as they do representing their companies. Prayer gatherings are lifting up missionaries, praying for people groups, studying new cultures, and equipping people to go with their blessing and support. Not everyone can go physically to all the world, but everyone can do something to help spread the gospel to those who have not heard it.

We can dig water wells, teach people how to plant crops, construct housing, send medical mission teams and equipment, and start orphanages; but every effort should be accompanied by preaching/teaching the gospel message in some form. The goal is greater than improving people's living conditions; the goal is giving them a chance to become born again and enter into the kingdom of God. If we can do both, wonderful. If we can't, choose to bring them into a relationship with Christ, and then He can begin to address the rest. "Seek first the kingdom of God and His righteousness, and all these things will be provided for you" (Matt. 6:33). The biblical principle tells us what our priorities need to be.

Fortunately, Christians are compassionate people who also make great efforts to improve the living conditions of those in developing countries, free people from slavery, help the trapped get out of prostitution and drug addictions, provide housing for the homeless, and a great many more important efforts. But the command is to "preach the gospel" and to "make disciples." We can do untold numbers of great things to help people; but if we have improved their lives without redeeming their souls, we have not fulfilled this command.

Application: Christ's commands are not optional for us. We are commanded to speak the gospel to those around us. We are commanded to share our faith in Christ, to affirm His lordship in our life, to bear witness to His resurrection in us as we are born again by His Spirit, and then to do all that is in our power to encourage others to do the same. Have you been faithfully sharing the good news with those yet in darkness? Your Lord expects it, He commands it, and He will be with you as you obey Him each step of the way. Consider now what your part is in taking the gospel to the entire world. Every person has a part to play, and your Lord is ready to reveal it to those who take His commands seriously. This task should not be disconcerting. It should be deeply fulfilling as we share the love of God with those who so desperately need to know it. It is an absolute joy to see lives transformed by the gospel message!

4. Feed My Lambs

- "When they had eaten breakfast, Jesus asked Simon Peter, 'Simon, son of John, do you love Me more than these?' 'Yes, Lord,' he said to Him, 'You know that I love you.' 'Feed My lambs,' He told him" (John 21:15).

John records an intimate, private conversation between Simon Peter and Jesus. It was a moment of restoration, reconciliation, redemption, and commission. Peter had failed Christ, abandoned Him at His arrest, and then three times denied even knowing Him.

But here, in this moment, Christ was opening Peter's eyes to a new calling—to care for those who needed the counsel and compassion of a spiritual leader. Jesus did not have an actual flock of sheep; but as the Good Shepherd, He has a multitude of followers today that need care and attention. A host of directives in the New Testament call us to care for one another; to serve one another; to consider others above ourselves; to take care of the weak, the young, and the vulnerable. And we are commanded, like Peter, to do our part in ministering to them.

Peter understood the importance of caring for the sheep and little lambs of Christ. He later wrote, "I exhort the elders among you: shepherd God's flock among you, not overseeing out of compulsion but freely, according to God's will; not for the money but eagerly; not lording it over those entrusted to you, but being examples to the flock. And when the chief Shepherd appears, you will receive the unfading crown of glory" (1 Pet. 5:1–4). This may reflect partly what Christ commanded in Matthew 28:20 to make disciples, "teaching them to observe everything I have commanded you." Certainly this would mean feeding them spiritually, but the term "feed" also included caring for, guiding, and shepherding. It means far more than preaching to them; it means loving them.

Although this command was directed to Peter, it applies to all of us in that we are to be concerned with the welfare of one another, disciple new believers, serve others, and teach and equip others for ministry. We, too, can feed and care for Christ's sheep as we care for one another.

Application: To feed lambs is to make every effort to care for our brothers and sisters in Christ, to counsel them, guide them, share biblical truths with them, pray for them, and walk beside them. Are you caring for others or most often just caring for yourself? How are you investing in the lives of others? Who are you walking alongside to encourage in the ways of the kingdom? Do not neglect the sheep of the Good Shepherd.

5. Demonstrate the Power of God

- "As you go, announce this: 'The kingdom of heaven has come near.' Heal the sick, raise the dead, cleanse those with skin diseases, drive out demons. You have received free of charge; give free of charge" (Matt. 10:7–8).

Some would say these commands are not for us today, that they were specifically for the disciples who were sent out to demonstrate the power of the gospel message. It is not difficult to accept that the first half of the command is valid, to preach; but it is the last half many have trouble with. The simple fact is, if Christ commands you to "heal the sick, raise the dead, cleanse those with skin diseases, and drive out demons," then you just have no option but to do it.

The key is in hearing from the Master. As you preach the gospel, various situations may arise, and it will be up to you to know how the Master is directing you. He did not ask us to heal all the world or cast demons out of everyone in the world, but He did ask us to take the gospel to every creature in the world. These other actions need great spiritual discernment. Christ has not changed. His power is no different now from what it was then. We do not presume upon the Lord as to what He wants us to do, but we also do not limit what we will allow Him to do through us. To Him be the glory, not us, in whatever we accomplish with His strength.

Got is not limited by physical constraints and neither are His people when they act in obedience to their Lord.

Application: Let the Lord lead you to use His power and strength to impact those in need around you. Some situations may truly call for a demonstration of God's power in order for the gospel message to penetrate the hearts of the hearers. Others may only need a quiet invitation to respond to Christ's love. Ask the Spirit to give you clear discernment and an awareness of His presence to lead and guide your actions to bring Him the glory and the praise in every situation.

6. Pray for God to Send Out Workers

- "Then He said to His disciples, 'The harvest is abundant, but the workers are few. Therefore, pray to the Lord of the harvest to send out workers into His harvest'" (Matt. 9:37–38).

This command is another one that reveals to us the character of God. It tells us what Peter wrote about, "The Lord does not delay His promise, as some understand delay, but is patient with you, not wanting any to perish, but all to come to repentance" (2 Pet. 3:9). The heart of God wills that no one should perish and spend an eternity apart from His presence. His desire for mankind is to bring them to repentance and a restored relationship with Himself so that they will not have to die in their sins. But it is God's plan to work through His people to bring this about.

Paul explains God's strategy: "For everyone who calls on the name of the Lord will be saved. But how can they call on Him in whom they have not believed? And how can they believe without hearing about Him? And how can they hear without a preacher? And how can they preach unless they are sent? As it is written: How beautiful are the feet of those who announce the gospel of good things!" (Rom. 10:13–15).

The message of the good news, the gospel, is not a gift to be hoarded but a gift to be shared openly with others. It is meant to be like leaven in bread, permeating the fabric of society; but it is dependent on those who have believed for its propagation. People do not spontaneously understand something they have never previously heard about. When we pray for God to send out laborers, we are, at the same time, offering our lives into His service where He has placed us. This command reveals to us the heart of God in order for us to align our hearts with His. We, too, should have a heart for the lost, a heart to share the good news, a heart to help the lost find their way home to God.

Application: When you pray this prayer for God to "send out workers into His harvest," whom does God bring to mind? Maybe a family member, an old friend, a people group or tribe who have not yet responded to the good news? Have you shared the gospel with them? Will you if you haven't?

7. Watch and Pray

- "Stay awake and pray so that you won't enter into temptation. The spirit is willing, but the flesh is weak" (Mark 14:38; also Luke 22:40).

This command was given to Christ's disciples on the evening He was arrested and eventually crucified. They were about to be tempted to deny knowing Christ, tempted to abandon Him to His enemies, tempted to flee instead of stay and fight, tempted to give in to their physical drowsiness and succumb to sleep. Christ knew they were about to face a whole series of temptations and so He exhorted them to watch and pray. But they did not. They *would* not. However willing they were in their minds, their bodies had more control; and as their eyelids closed, Christ's enemies drew nearer and nearer. Suddenly they awoke to fiery torches, gleaming spears and swords, temple henchmen, and pompous religious leaders all around, with Judas standing right in the middle. Each of the disciples gave in to their cowardice and fled into the night, cowering in dark places for fear of their own lives.

It would be easy to dismiss this as a particular command given only to the disciples, but the truth contained within it applies to every believer. The fact of the matter is that our spirit is indeed willing and desires to follow Christ. We want to serve Him, obey Him, love Him, seek after Him, worship Him, and know Him intimately. But our flesh is weak. No matter how many times we make resolutions, rededications, or commitments, no matter how often we surrender to Christ's lordship, we seem to fail. The key to success is to watch and pray. When we fail to watch and pray, we allow our flesh to win over our spirit.

Further, the disciples did not know what was about to happen despite the many times Christ had foretold this night would happen. He did not tell them His enemies were approaching; He told them to watch and pray. As they prayed and watched, they might have found courage, wisdom, spiritual insight, and an opportunity to support and encourage Christ before He was led away, mocked, tortured, and killed.

When we are watching and praying and seeking the Lord daily, we should never be caught off guard with what the day brings. Christ is happy to help prepare us mentally and spiritually for whatever comes our way. Those who spend their time engaging in worldly pursuits do not have their minds centered on Christ. They will be caught off guard, and their faith can be easily shaken. Any follower of Christ must be ready for action, prepared for any occasion, alert and watching for any indication from the Master.

The command still stands: *watch and pray*. Peter says, "Be serious! Be on the alert! Your adversary the Devil is prowling around like a roaring lion, looking for anyone he can devour" (1 Pet. 5:8). Giving in to temptation is the quickest way to deny Christ, to leave the path of righteousness, to abandon spiritual loyalties, and to self-destruct. Paul knew how important it was to stay alert and pray. He said, "Pray at all times in the Spirit with every prayer and request, and stay alert in this with all perseverance and intercession for all the saints" (Eph. 6:18). The prayers of the saints sustained him and gave him the strength to stand up under many trials and tribulations.

Christ warned that there would be times of great distress for believers prior to His return. He told them the day would come, and that most people would be unprepared for it, so His followers were to "be on your guard, so that your minds are not dulled from carousing, drunkenness, and worries of life, or that day will come on you unexpectedly like a trap. For it will come on all who live on the face of the whole earth. But be alert at all times, praying that you may have strength to escape all these things that are going to take place and to stand before the Son of Man" (Luke 21:34–36).

Application: What is your greatest temptation? What is the greatest threat to you stepping off the narrow road and onto the broad way? Guard your heart so that you will stand up under pressures to conform to the world and abandon your pursuit of godliness. Would you consider yourself to be a Christian who is "alert" to the Spirit of God? Do you see yourself as one who is "watching and praying"? Or, are you more likely distracted by the interests you have in the world and only occasionally aware of God's presence? The benefit of a regular devotional time of prayer is that you become practiced being in the presence of God, and He regularly has your undivided attention. Ask God today if He considers you to be a soldier who is always alert and prepared for action, or if you are a servant who is off doing his own thing while the Master is unable to get his attention.

8. Be Ready

- "You also be ready, because the Son of Man is coming at an hour that you do not expect" (Luke 12:40).
- "Therefore be alert, since you don't know what day your Lord is coming. But know this: If the homeowner had known what time the thief was coming, he would have stayed alert and not let his house be broken into. This is why you also must be ready, because the Son of Man is coming at an hour you do not expect" (Matt. 24:42–44).

Christ is coming back. This was His promise to those who follow Him and to those who don't. Unfortunately, too many Christians live like they believe He will not return during their lifetime. When we know company is coming to our home, we make the necessary preparations such as cleaning, cooking, clearing our schedules. But preparing for the coming of the Lord is far more serious and important.

Several parables Christ taught had to do with masters leaving on long journeys and returning to see how their servants had managed in their absence (Matt. 24:46, 50; 25:14; Mark 13:35; Luke 12:36–47). In one sense Christ has gone on a long journey and will return to see how we have been managing without His physical presence. The difference, however, is that He has provided us with

His Spirit to guide, protect, teach, and empower us to do His will in the meantime.

How and *when* He comes back is not as important as that He *is* coming back. When He returns, each one of us will stand before Him to give an account of the stewardship of our lives, our gifts and talents, and how we used our time and resources for His kingdom. He alone is our Judge, and as the gatekeeper to heaven, He determines who has been faithful and who has not.

We all long to hear the phrase, "Well done, good and faithful slave! You were faithful. . . . Share your master's joy!" (Matt. 25:21). When Christ returns, we need to be found with our hand to the plow rather than missing in action. Being ready means being diligent, staying focused, and not compromising our tasks assigned to us by our Master.

Application: It is easy to become complacent in the Christian life and turn our interests to worldly pursuits, focus on worldly cares, and become distracted by worldly issues. Christ commands us to be ready, to be alert, not to be distracted or have our attentions drawn away from kingdom matters. We are not to be fair-weather disciples, emerging from our distractions only when it suits us. When Christ returns, when His Spirit moves, will He find us standing at our posts or shirking our responsibilities?

9. Don't Worry about How to Witness

- "But when they hand you over, don't worry about how or what you should speak. For you will be given what to say at that hour, because you are not speaking, but the Spirit of your Father is speaking through you" (Matt. 10:19–20).
- "Whenever they bring you before synagogues and rulers and authorities, don't worry about how you should defend yourselves or what you should say. For the Holy Spirit will teach you at that very hour what must be said" (Luke 12:11–12).

This command relates to the previous one. It also reveals to us that the Father has provided us with a way to share the gospel message wherever He sends us. Our confidence is not to be in our own abilities or in our own preparation and strategy for witnessing; it is to be completely in the Lord. In fact, Christ tells us that our presentation of the good news should be a natural and ordinary part of our life, something we should not even worry about.

What is incredibly encouraging is that we have an opportunity to let God actually speak through us. We are simply instruments in His hands, a mouthpiece that His Spirit will use to speak truth to those around us. This is a relief to many who always seem to say the wrong things or who always second-guess themselves or feel there was so much more they could have said. The point is that

God will do all the talking if we can let Him have first place in our lives and if we can step out of His way and let Him penetrate the hearts of our hearers with His Spirit. If you put His Word in your heart, He will be able to draw it out of you in the right way and at the right time.

God is not looking for a fancy talking, well-trained orator; He is looking for a person who loves Him and who is willing to share that love with others whenever God gives the opportunity to do so. Be prepared to share clearly and concisely, and God will bring the opportunities along during the ordinariness of your day.

Application: Take time to put God's Word in your heart. Study to show yourself an approved workman of God. "Be diligent to present yourself approved to God, a worker who doesn't need to be ashamed, correctly teaching the word of truth" (2 Tim. 2:15). The degree to which you are prepared for service will determine your usefulness to God in His kingdom.

6

Cautions

I have come so that they may have life and
have it in abundance.

John 10:10

Christ has the ability and the authority to give life to anyone He chooses. "Just as the Father raises the dead and gives them life, so the Son also gives life to anyone He wants to" (John 5:21). This is not just talking about a normal living and breathing life; it is significantly more. Christ has every intention of helping His followers experience above and beyond what any normal life has to offer—everlasting joy, peace that goes beyond our understanding, hope beyond measure, and the filling presence of the Holy Spirit in our life.

When Christ promised us "abundant" life, it was not like the promises some politicians give to get elected—well-intentioned but empty. However, it *is* a conditional promise. Abundant life is promised only to those who lovingly follow His commands, thereby demonstrating His lordship in their life. Those who want to have an abundant life but do not follow Christ's commands will be disappointed and even get frustrated with God. The apostle Peter advises us, "As obedient children, do not be conformed to the desires of your former ignorance. But as the One who called you is holy, you also are to be holy in all your conduct; for it is written, Be holy, because I am holy. And if you address as Father the One who judges impartially based on each one's work, you are to conduct yourselves in reverence during the time of your temporary residence" (1 Pet. 1:14–17).

Christ wants us to use the abundant life He offers us wisely and with great care, and not use it recklessly or wastefully. In addition, He intends for us to experience the fullness of life not just here on the earth but for all eternity. We were created for eternity, not just for a temporary life here on the earth. We should always live today like we were in the presence of the Lord.

Fortunately, Christ's commands also provide us cautionary insights that help us avoid the pitfalls and entrapments that prevent us from experiencing abundant life. Jesus knows our weaknesses and our limits in withstanding temptations. He always provides us ways and means to stay on the path that leads to righteousness so we will not venture onto the road that leads us into destruction (1 Cor. 10:13). Look at the following commands as means to experience joy, peace, hope, and purpose as you live in God's presence.

1. Don't Be Anxious

- "This is why I tell you: Don't worry about your life, what you will eat or what you will drink; or about your body, what you will wear. Isn't life more than food and the body more than clothing?" (Matt. 6:25).
- "Therefore don't worry about tomorrow, because tomorrow will worry about itself. Each day has enough trouble of its own" (Matt. 6:34; also Luke 12:22ff).

An anxious person is a faithless person. The more people worry, the less they trust in God. To be anxious means to be consumed by a problem and allow it continually to dominate your thoughts. Worrying about things is an unproductive mental exercise that rarely, if ever, makes any difference in a situation.

The most effective antidote to worry is to take action. And as Christians we are to take our concerns to God and leave them there, not take them back up and continue to worry about them all day long. Christ wants us to believe that He cares for us. He wants us to place our faith in Him and trust He will take up our cause, deal with our problems, and intervene in our circumstances. Will we trust Him? Will we allow Him the time He needs to work things out in His way rather than trying to control our own destiny?

Not too long ago I was under tight financial constraints. We had moved home from overseas, spent all our savings on getting into a house, buying appliances, and a family car. Christmas was coming, even as car insurance, mortgage payments, and other obligations were becoming overwhelming to me. I could not see any clear way through the financial demands that were piling up on us. We were financially on the edge, and I felt like we were being pulled under with no one to throw a lifeline.

While speaking at a conference in another city, I found myself one night in my hotel room having trouble breathing. My chest felt constricted, my throat seemed to be closing, and I began to panic. I even wrote a good-bye letter to my family in case I did not make it through the night. Then I called my physician back home to see me immediately when I arrived home the next day (if I made it).

A heart stress test determined I was physically fine, but this gave only small relief. I went home and sat in my living room with the lights out, wondering how in the world I was going to get through the next few months. Then God said to me, "How dare you stand in pulpits preaching to people to trust in Me when you can't even do it yourself! Either quit preaching or start trusting!" I confessed my lack of trust to God, gave my family finances over to Him, and began to de-escalate from my state of anxiety. In the next five weeks, God brought $12,000 that covered all of our expenses and reminded me that there is nothing too big for God.

Paul reminds us of this command in his letter to the church in Philippi: "Don't worry about anything, but in everything, through prayer and petition with thanksgiving, let your requests be made known to God" (Phil. 4:6). The combination of taking our concerns to God and adding thanksgiving to it frees us from anxiety. The thanksgiving is our affirmation to God that we trust Him to handle our requests. If we can thank God that He has heard our prayers and thank Him for how He is going to answer them, we can then rest in Him, and His peace can cover us and keep us safe from worry.

Application: A life of worry is a wasted life. A life of trust is a blessed life. Christ's command encourages us to be blessed and to trust Him and His love for us. Ask the Spirit of God to remind you of His faithfulness, His provisions, His protection, His guidance, and His strength each time you begin to become anxious about your life or circumstances. Remember, He cares for you very much. What is stressing you out the most right now? What do you have the most trouble releasing into God's hands? What do you think Christ thinks about your control issues? Remember, when you are in control of your life, Christ isn't.

2. Handle Holy Things with Care

- "Don't give what is holy to dogs or toss your pearls before pigs, or they will trample them with their feet, turn, and tear you to pieces" (Matt. 7:6).

Whatever God gives us is always precious and holy and comes from His love for us. The gospel came to us at great price to Him because of His desire for us to be reconciled to Him. The truths we know from God's Word are promises revealed to us by His Spirit because we are His children. To treat the truths we have been given carelessly, to mishandle the Word of God, and to mismanage the resources God has entrusted into our care is like throwing a golden ring or ruby necklace into a pig sty and thinking the pigs may enjoy it, or dropping it into a dog food dish.

- Arguing over Christianity with atheists who are determined to destroy your faith is largely futile.
- Giving your God-given money to those who will immediately buy drugs or use it for gambling is reckless.
- Spending precious time with those who manipulate and abuse you benefits no one and wastes your time.
- Lending your car to a reckless driver who will abuse your kindness is more than foolish.

This command addresses several things. First, it helps us realize we need to be careful how we treat what God has given us.

I would not give my children into the care of anyone who would abuse or neglect them; neither would I give to others anything they would use recklessly or with disregard. This command helps us to be good stewards of the resources we have, the gifts we have been given, and the time we have, using them in a way that brings glory to Him and is not wasted on those who will immediately abuse, misuse, or cannot appreciate them.

Second, we are to be wise in our dealings with others, not careless or foolish or wasteful for the sake of being "Christians." Jesus was no pushover at the hands of the strong. He was no doormat others walked over. He was kind but firm. He was brutally honest toward hypocrites and directly confronted those who manipulated others for personal gain (Matt. 23). He was the protector of the weak, the advocate for the poor, the guide to the blind, and stood up to those who took advantage of others. Anyone who could willingly submit to being crucified on a Roman cross was not weak in any way whatsoever. Neither should we be. Gentle? Yes. Kind? Always. Merciful? Of course. But *not weak,* because we have Christ who abides in us, and He is not weak or frail.

Not giving in to the dogs or swine takes courage. They can be demanding, demeaning, and demoralizing, but we must remember, "You are from God, little children, and you have conquered them, because the One who is in you is greater than the one who is in the world" (1 John 4:4).

Application: We should not put undue importance on our belongings, but if what we have is misused and destroyed by one person, it will no longer be available to be used in ministry to others either. The time wasted with an unappreciative person could have been better spent with others in greater need. Ask God to give you spiritual discernment and His wisdom to know how to use your time and your resources wisely. Do not be manipulated or pressured by others to follow their priorities and urgencies. Let God guide you to be the best steward of what He has given you at all times. There is always a right time to share the gospel and minister to the needy. It should not be on their agenda but on God's.

3. Don't be Afraid of Persecution

- "Don't fear those who kill the body but are not able to kill the soul; rather, fear Him who is able to destroy both soul and body in hell" (Matt. 10:28; Luke 12:4).

Too often we are intimidated by those who oppose the gospel message or by godless people who may be in authority over us. As God's representatives, there is truly only one person we ever need to fear, and that is the One to whom we must one day give an account of our lives, God Himself.

None can compare in might or grandeur or power to the Lord God Almighty—*none!* When we speak and when we go, we do so according to His will; and we can be assured His power, wisdom, strength, and might will be afforded to us. Like Peter attempting to walk on water, when we take our eyes off our Lord and look to the surrounding tempest, we begin to fear. This command should give us great comfort in that the One we are told to fear is also the One who loves us most.

When we lose our fear of God, we begin to go astray. When we take sin lightly, we have lost our fear of God. When we knowingly sin or disobey God, giving in to our lust and desire, we have lost our fear of God. When we willfully engage in ongoing sinful activities and behaviors, we have lost our fear of God.

Losing our fear of God will at first bring chastisement and then lead to punishment and eventually judgment if we do not repent and return to God. The ultimate punishment outlined in this command is being destroyed both body and soul in hell. This is what is reserved for those who have no fear of God. They may not fear God now, but they will experience perpetual terror for all of eternity when they die.

This command gives guidance, a warning, and the consequence of disobeying the command. David shows a healthy understanding and appreciation for the fear of the Lord in what he wrote:

- "The LORD is my light and my salvation—whom should I fear? The LORD is the stronghold of my life—of whom should I be afraid?" (Ps. 27:1).
- "Now the eye of the LORD is on those who fear Him—those who depend on His faithful love" (Ps. 33:18).
- "The Angel of the LORD encamps around those who fear Him, and rescues them" (Ps. 34:7).
- "The fear of the LORD is the beginning of wisdom; all who follow His instructions have good insight. His praise endures forever" (Ps. 111:10).

Application: If there is any person you fear more than you fear God, that says more about your view of God than how strong the other person is. You must remember that "the One who is in you is greater than the one who is in the world" (1 John 4:4). You have all of God residing inside of you when you are a believer. All of His power, might, strength, and wisdom. Let God be your defender, and you focus on being faithful. Is there any chance that you have lost your fear of God? If you are waiting to see if God notices that you are living a life that challenges His expectations for you, you can expect Him to respond in a loving but firm manner in the days to come. But at some point, His patience will turn to judgment if there is no repentance. The best chance to avoid the impending consequences of your sin is to repent quickly and confess your sins now. He is faithful and just and will forgive you completely, but the consequences of your sin may remain.

4. Do Not Fear

- "Your heart must not be troubled. Believe in God; believe also in Me" (John 14:1).
- "Peace I leave with you. My peace I give to you. I do not give to you as the world gives. Your heart must not be troubled or fearful" (John 14:27).

Many times throughout Scripture God commands His people not to be afraid. For those who honor Him, there is never a need to fear or to be anxious. When we are in right relationship with God, following His commands and loving Him with our heart, soul, strength, and mind, we rest content in His protection and control over the situations in our life. Yes, we will face trials, difficult circumstances, tragedy, and stressful times, but despite all of it, we can have inner peace—even joy—knowing whose we are. Paul says it this way:

- "I am able to do all things through Him who strengthens me" (Phil. 4:13).
- "No, in all these things we are more than victorious through Him who loved us" (Rom. 8:37).

And Christ reminds us:

- "I have told you these things so that in Me you may have peace. You will have suffering in the world. Be courageous! I have conquered the world" (John 16:33).

- "When I saw Him, I fell at His feet like a dead man. He laid His right hand on me and said, 'Don't be afraid! I am the First and the Last, and the Living One. I was dead, but look—I am alive forever and ever, and I hold the keys of death and Hades'" (Rev. 1:17–18).

The challenge is to believe in Christ when the storms begin to swirl around us. With so much incredible power living within us and the promised victory He gives us, a lack of faith will steal from us the peace Christ promises us. When, like Peter, we take our eyes off Christ and look to our circumstances, we begin to sink in the midst of the storm (Matt. 14:30).

Before Christ came to the earth, we had God alone to believe in to take care of our needs. But here Christ expands belief to Himself as He equates Himself with God in power and strength. Together with the Spirit, they create a formidable powerhouse of strength on our behalf. To doubt their ability to sustain us is to doubt their love for us and to question their ability in the face of life's storms. When we see any situation or circumstance as more powerful than God or as unconquerable in our eyes, it reveals just how small our faith really is.

Application: Are there any circumstances or situations you believe have greater power than God has in your life? Are there people in your life that you feel are too far gone for even God to redeem? Are there habits, addictions, or compulsions you have stopped fighting and given in to because you do not believe God has the power to overcome them in your life? If so, you may want to ask God to forgive your faithlessness and your doubt in His ability to demonstrate His power and love to you.

5. Do Not Be Deceived

- "Then He said: 'Watch out that you are not deceived. For many will come in My name, saying, "I am the Messiah," and they will deceive many. You are going to hear of wars and rumors of wars. See that you are not alarmed, because these things must take place, but the end is not yet'" (Luke 21:8–9; also Matt. 24:4–5).

Being deceived means to be manipulated, lied to, or being under control of someone with nefarious intentions. It can also mean being deluded or living with a false reality. In the Lord's Prayer, Christ prays that we would be delivered from temptation and kept from the evil one (Matt. 6:13). He does not want His people to be deceived, tricked, blindsided, or compromised because of false teachings, deceptive arguments, or counterfeit Christians. In fact, many people have come and will continue to come pretending to be either Christ Himself or messengers/prophets/teachers of Christ in an attempt to gain a following. In order not to be deceived by false teachers, false leaders, and wolves in sheep's clothing, you must be spiritually wise and biblically discerning.

The only way to obtain godly wisdom is to have God's Spirit living and active in your life. He is the One who will reveal truth in difficult situations and protect your heart and mind from the evil one. "When the Spirit of truth comes, He will guide you into all the truth. For He will not speak on His own, but He will speak whatever He hears. He will also declare to you what is to come" (John 16:13). Only those who do not know the truth can be deceived. Falsehood is always revealed in the light of truth.

There is another spirit in the world—the spirit of darkness and deceit: "We know that we are of God, and the whole world is under the sway of the evil one" (1 John 5:19). And we must guard our hearts from being deceived, even in small ways. The primary means of growing in our knowledge and in truth is through study and meditating on God's Word, the Bible. It is the only source of pure truth apart from God Himself (Father, Son, and Spirit). Those who refuse to spend time in God's Word are the most susceptible to deception and can be easily swayed to false teachings and fraudulent leaders. Seek God's truth, be filled with the Spirit of God, and study the Word of God; and you will quickly be able to identify false teachers and false teachings.

Application: Be diligent in your study of God's Word and continually be filled with the Spirit of God so that you will not easily be deceived by the evil one. Christ defeated the temptations of Satan by knowing God's Word. Don't be unarmed and unprepared for battle when it comes upon you. Truth is your only weapon against the lies of Satan and the pressures of society. When you have God in your life (Father, Son, and Spirit), you will have truth resident in you (John 14:6). Ask God to show you if you have been deceived by anyone or if you are adhering to any false doctrines or theologies. Let His Spirit purge you from all falsehood and replace it with His truth.

6. Don't Be Afraid of Suffering

- "Don't be afraid of what you are about to suffer. Look, the Devil is about to throw some of you into prison to test you, and you will have affliction for 10 days. Be faithful until death, and I will give you the crown of life" (Rev. 2:10).

Christ knew what His people were about to face. They would encounter suffering that would challenge their faith. Some would be thrown into prison, and many would die. This was a daunting truth for believers to have to face, but their confidence and trust were in their Lord.

Facing suffering without fear is no easy task unless you already happen to know the outcome. If you understand that suffering is the only way to achieve success and victory, then it can be well worth the pain. Christ was able to endure the cross because He knew victory was coming three days later. The cost was worth providing reconciliation between a lost humanity and His Father in heaven.

But if the suffering is pointless and there is no greater good to be achieved, then there is good reason to fear. Had Christ not had any guarantee of being raised from the dead and being seated at the right hand of His Father or if Christ did not know His death had any purpose, there would have been no reason for Him to endure such suffering.

Christ offers a crown of life for those who pay the ultimate price for their faithfulness. But we can be confident in knowing any suffering we endure is temporary. We also know that Christ is fully able to understand our suffering as He also endured the ultimate suffering on the cross. He will walk with us in the midst of our suffering and bring glory to Himself in the end as we remain faithful.

Application: Facing suffering requires dependency on our Lord. It brings necessary growth and depth in our relationship with Him, and it forces us to put our priorities in proper order, causing us to use our time and resources with great care. Suffering is not caused by God, but God allows it and uses it to mold and shape us into vessels that are increasingly more valuable and usable to Him. In the midst of suffering, keep your eyes on the Author and Finisher of your faith so that when you come through it your faith will shine more brightly. Suffering is not fun, challenging, useful, praiseworthy, or desirable; it is suffering. You may come to the place where you question God's love for you, or whether it is worth standing firm in your faith. That is the point where you will cry to the Lord and He will hear you and come and join you, walk with you, and carry you through it to victory. You can have victory even in the midst of pain and trials knowing you are in the hands of God.

7. Strengthen What's Left, Hold on to What You Have

- "Be alert and strengthen what remains, which is about to die, for I have not found your works complete before My God. Remember, therefore, what you have received and heard; keep it, and repent. But if you are not alert, I will come like a thief, and you have no idea at what hour I will come against you" (Rev. 3:2–3).
- "I am coming quickly. Hold on to what you have, so that no one takes your crown" (Rev. 3:11).

Whether they knew it or not, the church in Sardis was in trouble. They had been neglecting what they had been taught and were living in disobedience to God and needed to repent. Whatever little they had left of what they had received and heard was about to die out. Christ here warned them to stop everything and strengthen what was left or it would be too late. Their priorities had shifted, their focus was off, and they were treading down a pathway of no return. Christ told them there was still time to save themselves from certain destruction, but the choice was theirs.

The church in Philadelphia seems to have fared better but was in danger of losing what they currently had and losing their reward for their faithfulness. Christ said to hold on tight to what they had, lest they lose out in the end. The warning here is to be careful not to let others distract us from our purpose, or steal our treasure, or take from us what is most precious. This church was on the right track but was vulnerable to their enemies. They were to put extra measures in place to protect and guard what they had in their possession, ensuring that no one could take it away from them.

The church in Sardis was facing the result of their own neglect and distraction, whereas the church in Philadelphia was facing potential outside attacks. Christ gave both churches a warning to protect what they had, nurture it, guard it, and fan it back into flame so that their church would not be in danger of dying.

Application: What would you say is most important in the life of your church? What would alter the character and direction of your church if it were taken away (fellowship, doctrine, ministry, leadership, etc.)? Be careful not to neglect the fundamentals: the two greatest commandments, modeling 1 Corinthians 13, authentic worship, in-depth Bible study and prayer, meaningful ministry to others, and faithful service to God. If you neglect the basics, you are in jeopardy of losing your focus, getting sidetracked on secondary issues, following after fads and gimmicks, and becoming ineffective and unusable to your Lord. Not only should you protect and hold on to what you have, but you must strengthen it so there is no chance of losing it and being rebuked by your Lord.

8. Beware of False Prophets

- "Beware of false prophets who come to you in sheep's clothing but inwardly are ravaging wolves" (Matt. 7:15).
- "Then Jesus told them, 'Watch out and beware of the yeast of the Pharisees and Sadducees'" (Matt. 16:6).

It is so sad when well-meaning people get so far off track in their lives that they cause harm and wreak havoc where originally they meant to do good. Many have been deceived and are blind to the harm they are causing God's people and God's kingdom; others do it deliberately and methodically.

Here Christ warns us of those who present and portray themselves as godly but are quite the opposite. They want to be accepted as spiritual leaders among God's people, but they have evil intentions and selfish desires. In time their fruit will make clear their evil heart because division, discord, strife, hurt, confusion, manipulation, and accusation follow them wherever they go. They may not stay long in any one place as their deeds find them out. Yet they continue on their destructive path deceiving, manipulating, and destroying God's people.

Something as simple as questioning the character and integrity of the pastor, constantly causing division during business meetings, bringing unjust accusations against godly leaders, teaching corrupt theology or doctrines to teenagers, pressuring or manipulating the church to go in unhealthy directions, and more—all have the same end to destroy the kingdom of God one church at a time. Web sites, books, radio programs, traveling preachers, conference leaders, and visitors should be vetted through wise and godly people to protect the body from wolves and subversive agents who can dash the faith of the unsuspecting, the gullible, and the young in the faith among your members.

Application: Do not easily accept new people into leadership, but test them for a good length of time to see if people are drawn closer to God through their work and ministry, or if they are drawn closer to the new person instead. See if they point people to Christ or to themselves. Do they cause people to question authority and become harsh or critical of others, or do they instead become more loving and supportive of the leadership? Be wise in how you accept outsiders in your midst, or your blind acceptance may lead to the demise of your church. Loyalty to a person should never supersede loyalty to the body of Christ. Protect the body of Christ; do the hard thing, or you may risk the destruction of the church body and face years of regret.

9. Don't Worry About Your Life

- "This is why I tell you: Don't worry about your life, what you will eat or what you will drink; or about your body, what you will wear. Isn't life more than food and the body more than clothing?" (Matt. 6:25; also Luke 12:22).

If there was ever a command that brings great comfort, it is this one. With economic downturns, catastrophic natural disasters, violent crimes, child molesters, unscrupulous money managers, health scares, worldwide outbreaks of disease, and political leaders devoid of any moral code of conduct, we can easily and rightfully be overcome, even paralyzed, with worry about life and what the future may bring. We are commanded not to worry about these things or anything else.

What a relief to be confidently able to trust our life into the hands of someone who truly loves us and who possesses the genuine power to intervene, protect, and guide us through the abundant land mines and aerial assaults of life. Also, what a contrast between the thief who "comes only to steal and to kill and to destroy" and the Good Shepherd who "lays down his life for His sheep" (John 10:10–11).

Exchanging worry for trust is not always easy. Some people believe unless they worry, they are not doing anything productive to solve their situation. But worry is a demonstration of lack of faith in God. Worry means you do not trust God to be able to handle your situations. Christ promises to provide His people with all that they need—the basics of food and clothing—and after that, everything else is a bonus. The more time you spend trying to take care of your own needs, the less time you have to focus on your ministry to others. Do what you can, and leave the rest to the Lord.

Application: Do you obsess over the latest fashions, the perfect makeup, cutting-edge hairstyles, reading all the newest house/clothing/style magazines? Why? What is the point? Do you spend an equal or greater amount of time reading your Bible, serving in ministry, praying, and worshipping God? How often do you have a spiritual fast and spend time in prayer that you would have spent cooking and eating? How you spend your time and what you think about most often reveals what is most important in your life. Christ wants you to know He plans to take care of the details of your life so you can concentrate on things that are more important. Add up the amount of time you will spend in food preparation, cooking, and clean-up, and compare it to the amount of time you spend in Bible study and prayer. Average how much time you spend shopping for clothes, reading fashion magazines, or looking at celebrities on Web sites, and compare it to the amount of time you spend in ministry to others. How do they compare?

10. Take Heed

- "Be careful not to practice your righteousness in front of people, to be seen by them. Otherwise, you will have no reward from your Father in heaven" (Matt. 6:1).

Christ had elaborated on this point earlier when He said, "For I tell you, unless your righteousness surpasses that of the scribes and Pharisees, you will never enter the kingdom of heaven" (Matt. 5:20). The righteousness of the scribes and Pharisees was based on external ritual and formal routine. It focused on gaining the applause of men and the recognition of the community because of their deliberately public show of piety and self-denial. On the outside they looked like model citizens. But on the inside they were empty, self-serving, and full of selfish ambition (Luke 11:39).

Entrance into Christ's kingdom requires a righteousness that begins on the inside and works to impact every aspect of one's life. It is not for show or approval of mankind but seeks to serve God alone. The aim of this righteousness is not an enhanced reputation in the community but to seek and find God Himself.

Those who seek man's approval, recognition, and affirmation will be the ones who declare before Christ on the day of judgment, "Lord, Lord, didn't we prophesy in Your name, drive out demons in Your name, and do many miracles in Your name?" (Matt. 7:22). Christ will look into their hearts, and He will see that they have already received their rewards. They had the applause of men. They had the admiration of the crowds. They had the places of importance at the receptions and the seats of honor at the banquet tables. They were spoken of highly by the community and given recognition by the influential in society. They got what they were looking for. But because they were not looking to please God, Christ "will announce to them, 'I never knew you! Depart from Me, you lawbreakers!'" (Matt. 7:23).

Christ provides the correction for His disciples: "But when you give to the poor, don't let your left hand know what your right hand is doing, so that your giving may be in secret. And your Father who sees in secret will reward you" (Matt. 6:3–4). We are able to choose our reward for our acts of righteousness. We can choose to be recognized and honored by the people around us, or we can choose to be recognized and honored by God who sees all that we are doing. The wise person always chooses to honor God and seeks His blessings and approval. Jesus should know—His one aim above all else was to please His Father in heaven (John 17:4).

Application: Our inside (heart) and our outside (actions) need to be the same; otherwise our service is for show and cannot bring glory to God. Take time before God today to let His Spirit evaluate your heart before Him. Ask Him to help you honor Him instead of trying to impress others around you.

11. Give God What Belongs to Him

- "Therefore give back to Caesar the things that are Caesar's, and to God the things that are God's" (Matt. 22:21; Luke 20:25).

This command was given in response to a question posed to Christ regarding whether one should pay taxes to the state. But the wisdom in His response is undeniable. Further, it clearly differentiates between our obligation to earthly powers and our obligation to heavenly powers. It also tells us that God is not threatened or particularly concerned by earthly powers because He is the One who permits them to exist in the first place. "Everyone must submit to the governing authorities, for there is no authority except from God, and those that exist are instituted by God. So then, the one who resists the authority is opposing God's command, and those who oppose it will bring judgment on themselves" (Rom. 13:1–2).

Paul goes on to say, "Pay your obligations to everyone: taxes to those you owe taxes, tolls to those you owe tolls, respect to those you owe respect, and honor to those you owe honor" (Rom. 13:7). Unless God directs us otherwise, standing against "Caesar" in this world is unproductive and can actually undermine the activity of God.

Christ wants His people to be "above reproach," meaning there should be nothing anyone can point to in your life that can be used to bring any accusation against you—no corruption, no slander, no deceitfulness, no drunkenness, no sexual impurity—including subversive activities against your government. There are times when God's people are directed by God to stand against evil government leaders, even bring down corrupt and evil regimes, but this must be done according to the guidance and power and wisdom of the Spirit of God if it is the effect God desires for it to have.

Application: Are you rendering properly those things that pertain to your own government, both federal and local? Too often religious "fanatics" are seen as enemies of the state because of their secretive, suspicious, antigovernment stances. Christians need to be open, above reproach, and model citizens doing what they can to help the government govern wisely and carefully. Do you pray regularly for those governing your city and country? God is big enough to raise up leaders and strong enough to remove them in due time. As we render to God what is rightfully His and are model citizens in His kingdom, He will show us what our role is to be as citizens of this world.

Epilogue

Following Christ's Commands Is an Act of Love

You did not choose Me, but I chose you. I appointed you that you should go out and produce fruit and that your fruit should remain, so that whatever you ask the Father in My name, He will give you.

JOHN 15:16

Christ chose us and ordained us to be fruitful, to exhibit the kind of fruit His Spirit brings forth in our lives: "love, joy, peace, patience, kindness, goodness, faith, gentleness, self-control" (Gal. 5:22–23). However, this also brings to mind those "works" that Christ foreordained that we should accomplish. "For we are His creation, created in Christ Jesus for good works, which God prepared ahead of time so that we should walk in them" (Eph. 2:10).

But it is impossible for us to do *either* of these—bear fruit that will last and accomplish all that God has prepared in advance for us to do—if we are not willing to follow His will for our lives. We cannot fulfill our purpose as His creation if we walk in disobedience to the commands of our Lord.

When we reject Christ's declared will for His people, we pull ourselves out of His will and create an alternate reality, one that functions without His guidance, Spirit, power, authority, peace, joy, protection, and wisdom. But when we lovingly choose to follow His commands, we immediately have access to all there is in Christ. We have the full measure of all the resources in the kingdom of God, including access to the King Himself.

Christ desires to make us a blessed people. He wants us to experience the joy of our salvation, the peace that passes understanding, the hope of His calling, and the fullness of His love in our lives. And this is why He has given us His commands. Jesus says, "If you know these things, you are blessed if you do them" (John 13:17).

Too many times we place a negative connotation on obedience. We bristle when someone demands that we follow the rules, like a dog in obedience school complying with the commands of its master. And yet over and over the Bible says that following and obeying God's commands is an experience connected by love, both our love for God and His love for us.

- "I, the LORD your God, am a jealous God, punishing the children for the fathers' sin, to the third and fourth generations of those who hate Me, but showing faithful love to a thousand generations of those who love Me and keep My commands" (Exod. 20:5–6).

- "Know that Yahweh your God is God, the faithful God who keeps His gracious covenant loyalty for a thousand generations with those who love Him and keep His commands" (Deut. 7:9).
- "Love the LORD your God and always keep His mandate and His statutes, ordinances, and commands" (Deut. 11:1).
- "If you carefully obey My commands I am giving you today, to love the LORD your God and worship Him with all your heart and all your soul, I will provide" (Deut. 11:13–14).
- "For I am commanding you today to love the LORD your God, to walk in His ways, and to keep His commands, statutes, and ordinances, so that you may live and multiply, and the LORD your God may bless you in the land you are entering to possess" (Deut. 30:16).
- "I delight in Your commands, which I love" (Ps. 119:47).
- "Only carefully obey the command and instruction that Moses the LORD's servant gave you: to love the LORD your God, walk in all His ways, keep His commands, remain faithful to Him, and serve Him with all your heart and all your soul" (Josh. 22:5).
- "The one who has My commands and keeps them is the one who loves Me. And the one who loves Me will be loved by My Father. I also will love him and will reveal Myself to him" (John 14:21).

- "If you keep My commands you will remain in My love, just as I have kept My Father's commands and remain in His love" (John 15:10).
- "This is how we know that we love God's children when we love God and obey His commands. For this is what love for God is: to keep His commands. Now His commands are not a burden" (1 John 5:2–3).

If we think that Christ's commands are too restrictive, too burdensome, too harsh, or too unreasonable, then we do not really know Christ at all. He is not vindictive, harsh, or uncaring; He is a loving, caring provider who desires to bless His people whenever possible. If we have trouble obeying Christ's commands, we will also have trouble loving Him.

Consider every obedience an act of love towards the One who gave His life for us. Consider every act of kindness shown to others as an act of kindness shown to Christ. Christ's commands are designed to develop our character, to help us treat others as He would treat them, to give us a heart like Christ's, and to help us keep our priorities in order. Obedience to His commands not only makes us people He can use in His kingdom, but people who will experience the life He created us to have in the first place.

So this is primarily a book about love. Jesus said, "If you love Me, you will keep My commands. . . . If anyone loves Me, he will keep My word. My Father will love him, and We will come to him and make Our home with him. The one who doesn't love Me will not keep My words" (John 14:15, 23–24).

Following the commands of Christ, simply put, is an act of love. A child of God cannot in one breath say, "I love you, Lord," and then turn around and disobey Christ's directives and expectations for His children. Love always leads to actions that demonstrate our love and prove it to be true.

Far too many people view the commands of God or the commands of Christ as restrictive or punitive—too many "thou shalt nots." But God is not giving us restrictions; He is giving us guidelines to help us avoid disaster and to free us from the bondage in which we might otherwise find ourselves. God's instructions for us are designed to help us prosper—in our relationships with others, in our quality of life, in our walk with Him, and in finding fulfillment and purpose in life.

> The LORD commanded us to follow all these statutes and to fear the LORD our God for our prosperity always and for our preservation, as it is today. Righteousness will be ours if we are careful to follow every one of these commands before the LORD our God, as He has commanded us. (Deut. 6:24–25)

Henry Blackaby states in his book *Experiencing God*, "God's commands are designed to guide you to life's best. You will not obey Him, however, if you do not believe Him or trust Him. You will not believe Him if you do not love him. You cannot love Him unless you know Him. But if you really come to know God as He reveals Himself to you, you will love Him. If you love Him, you will believe and trust Him. If you believe and trust Him, you will obey Him."

May you find the joy, peace, hope, and love God intended for you when He sent His Son to show us the way back into His presence and reveal to us the pathway of righteousness.